THE WHITE MAN'S BURDEN

Judith Bogod

Copyright © 2017 by Judith Bogod
judyb.200@gmail.com

All rights reserved. No part of this publication may be reproduced, stored in a retrieval system, or transmitted, in any form or by any means, electronic, mechanical, photocopying, recording, or otherwise, without the written prior permission of the publisher.

ISBN 978-0-9958727-0-7

For more information contact Judith at judyb.200@gmail.com

Typeset in *Caslon*.

Printed in Canada by Printorium Bookworks / Island Blue, Victoria B.C.

Dedication

Thank you to Philip, my spouse, lover and friend of fifty-five years, my proofreader and resource for my hopeless logic, and computer ineptness. Thank you for your many suggestions to bring this book to life. It comes with an apology for my long absences from the kitchen during the many hours I was obsessed with writing.

Thank you to my two older children, Nicholas and Karen, for your resilience and unwavering goodwill as you moved from country to country, school to school. That today you retain interesting recollections of your childhood years in South Africa speaks to the value of the decision we made to leave England for two years in South Africa. My younger daughter, Elizabeth, barely one year old when we left for South Africa, of course, had no recollections. She would often express regret that she had not been older.

The White Man's Burden

Thanks to Sheila Martindale, published poet, for editing and rectifying my acquired life-time British habit of putting the period and comma outside quotation marks when Canadian punctuation rules dictate the reverse.

It has been on my bucket list to write a book since at eighteen I did not pursue my dream to become a newspaper reporter. At the time, compensation for a trainee newspaper reporter was three pounds a week or it might have been a month. Either way, my parents considered it an insult, it being the olden days and them having the ruling hand, any career as a lowly paid newspaper reporter was ruled out. However, in truth, as my own person, the reason I rejected the idea had nothing to do with remuneration. It was the result of a school education trip to London's Daily Mirror where I was repulsed by the sight of half-eaten, yucky, greasy bacon and cheese rolls in various stages of decay, sickening and disgusting, on the desks of its reporters in the News Room. While to become a reporter then was a three-year indenture at three pounds a week or month, not a four-year university journalism degree, there was at least a chance of a job.

This is not a history book. It is simply a slice in the life of one family. To my grandchildren, Stori, Tatum, Lucie, Eve and Kate, your mother and father were your age when they spent two years in South Africa. I hope one day you may find it of interest.

Now it is done, what's next?

To Lesley

The best neighbour in Topaz

Judith Sept 2017

"There is no passion to be found playing small –
in settling for a life that is less than the one you are
capable of living."

NELSON MANDELA

Preface

I can well understand why the title of this book might be perceived as racist. For this reason, I feel I should add further context to explain the choice of title. This is the story of one family during two years of the forty-six year regime of Apartheid, a time when three million white South Africans held political and economic sway over twenty-two million blacks in a system of radical racism called Apartheid. The effect of this racism was to oppress, subjugate, discriminate and dehumanize the black majority population. I want to assure readers that the whole tenor of this book speaks strongly against the horror, the injustice and the indignity of racial discrimination and the wrongfulness of the Apartheid regime that put millions of black South Africans into abject slavery in their own land.

I first heard the phrase 'The White Man's Burden' in a South African family doctor's office while registering as new patient. I overheard the receptionist, a very pregnant white English South

The White Man's Burden

African, speaking about her imminent need for a nanny. In passing conversation, I mentioned to her how good my maid was with my baby daughter. This evoked the comment: "Oh, you'll know the white man's burden, then." Taken aback and not comprehending the significance of the remark, I let it pass. I heard this same phrase the second time from our landlord, a politician and freedom fighter, speaking about how he felt an ethical burden to give a job to a black South African because of the millions of unemployed black South Africans. He employed a full-time maid and garden boy despite the fact he had no need of their services.

The third time was the bizarre notion expressed by white Afrikaners that the administration of Bantu education, the Homelands, the Townships, the Bantu police force, was a financial burden they bore with patience and endurance. Totally overlooked in the equation was the cheap labor provided by those twenty-two million blacks to oil the wheels of South Africa's booming economy and enable the white Afrikaner to luxuriate in the highest standard of living in the world. "Kaffir boy, bring my boots" pretty well says it all.

There was a fourth burden too. The black maid became a member of the family, another daughter as it were, with all the obligations that went with it, the doctor, the dentist, the lawyer, optometrist, the funeral for a cousin, settling credit debts, schooling for her children, Christmas and birthday gifts, clothes, a pension for a long-standing, beloved servant too old to work. The National Government provided no free medicine, unemployment benefit or state pension for black workers. A South African friend of mine, who left during Apartheid for the UK, said she worried how her black maid who had worked for her thirty years would survive. Before leaving the country, she arranged for a sum of money to be paid monthly to her elderly maid so she could live out her days in relative comfort. Such necessities were burdened on those white employers who felt compassionate enough to accept them as a moral and humane responsibility.

The massive black population living in dire poverty and subjugation was an ever present threat to the Afrikaners' language, their history, their God, their very existence, a time bomb in waiting for insurrection. In 1979, to be fair, there were some white Afrikaners who could foresee an ever evolving multi-cultural world and the looming demise of Apartheid. By juxtaposition, there were English-speaking white South Africans ecstatic in their paradise oblivious and untroubled at piggybacking for personal gain on the impoverished black people. There were hard-line white Afrikaners as well as hard-line white English South Africans and, to add complexity to the mix, there were open-minded, empathetic, white-speaking South Africans of UK and European heritage horrified by the system of blatant, inhuman racism but powerless to make change.

In early psychology, students learn Abraham Maslow's Theory of Human Development. This theory depicts, in ladder form, the stages needed for self-actualization, a mystifying word but one I interpret to mean the attainment of freedom, pride of self, absolute self-fulfillment and complete happiness. In 1978-1979, I could not put the black South African on any one rung of this ladder. The Afrikaner political regime ruled through power and economic advantage solely for its own benefit. Afrikaner racism ignored the fundamental needs of humanity for safety, food, shelter and employment, all components of the Maslow Theory.

The White Man's Burden

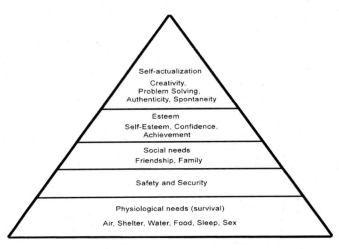

Maslow's Theory of Human Development

Cartoonists and satirists over the years have sought to draw attention to social wrongs through use of humor. The inclusion in this book of humor and tongue in cheek innuendo is not intended in any way to diminish the gravity of forty-six years of Apartheid. The satire and humor in this book are purely to "help a spoonful of sugar make the medicine go down."

DAY BY DAY   by Abe Berry

**This book is a work of non-fiction.
Some names have been changed for reasons of confidentiality.**

Time and memory may have faded some facts.

The photographs in this book date from 1979/9. In 1978 cameras were not the see and click technological marvels they are today. Images were captured on film, processed through a chemical tank in a darkened room, the finished product often half a head or totally blank. A roll of 20 photographs might see two or three usable pictures. In the circumstances, I request readers' forbearance when asked to stand on their heads to view some of the photographs in this book!

Prologue

Victoria, British Columbia, Canada, 2013

When I am at home by myself, I like to have the radio on. It is a way for a busy housewife to update herself on news, both world and local. I catch snippets of conversation as I move from room to room, making beds, vacuuming, Windexing bathroom mirrors, and disinfecting toilets. Radio hosts, Frank Stanford or Al Ferraby, fill the silence in my house much like having coffee at the neighbors. My last port of call is the kitchen where I do advance preparation for the evening meal, peeling spuds, cutting vegetables, defrosting meat or fish for the family to sit down to a wholesome dinner. The radio, now plainly audible, intones about Alice Munro and the art of the short story.

About half way through the morning by force of habit, I yearn for that which the British familiarly call 'elevenses', a mid-morning coffee to 'stimulate the phagocytes', a euphemism attached to me like an ear-worm from Bernard Shaw's The Doctor's Dilemma, to whit, a magical cure for all ills. In this case, the ill

The White Man's Burden

was a simple one, the need for caffeine to boost my energy, readily available in a cup of coffee. In the kitchen, the radio talk is now about protesters in the Ukraine demanding the resignation of their President. Lifting the steaming mug to my lips, I hear, "We interrupt this broadcast to bring you breaking news. South Africa's President, Jacob Zuma, announced the death of Nelson Mandela last night at the age of 95." I put down my coffee. It is Thursday, December 5th, 2013. Madiba is dead. The news of Madiba's death resonates deeply with me. I had never met him. I live six thousand miles away. Why?

It is September 1978. I am in Cape Town, South Africa. I am a young mother at the top of Table Mountain gazing across a calm Atlantic Ocean. Out to sea, I notice a small island. I point it out to Philip. "Robben Island" he says "where Nelson Mandela is in jail for treason".

Apartheid should never have happened but it did.

I lived through a mere two years of the story. I did not make history nor even put a dent in it, but in a very tiny way I feel I have left a footprint. I am reminded of the parable of the man walking a sandy beach one morning after a storm.

> *In the distance, he could see someone moving like a dancer. As he came closer, he saw that it was a young woman picking up starfish and gently throwing them into the ocean. "Young lady, why are you throwing starfish into the ocean?" "The sun is up and the tide is going out and, if I do not throw them into the ocean, they will die," she said. "But young lady, do you not realize that there are many miles of beach and thousands of*

starfish? You cannot possibly hope to make a difference." The young woman listened politely, then bent down, picked up a starfish and threw it into the sea. "It made a difference for this one," she replied.

I feel a connection with the lady on the beach. I made a difference in the lives of twenty-three starfish; the three people with black skins who lived in my employ and the twenty unemployed black maids and garden boys to whom I taught housekeeping, cooking and garden-care to prepare them for employment. Mine was a miniscule intervention in the big picture, a simple expression of common human decency but it was at a time when kindness and compassion were at a premium. I like to think of myself as proxy South African and am so thankful for the miracle that saw the South Africa I love freed from bondage without bloodshed.

The Rainbow Nation has taken its rightful place in the world and all of us are the richer for its traditions, culture, keen sportsmanship, happy, smiley faces, voices raised in proud harmony to the new National Anthem, 'Nkosi Sikelel iAfrika.'

To its black, colored and white peoples, its entire peoples, South Africa, it is good to have you back.

Table of Contents

Preface vii

Prologue xiii
Victoria, British Columbia, Canada, 2013

1   London, UK 1
December 1977

2   Arrival 15
Johannesburg, South Africa January 19, 1978

3   Settling In 27

4   About Maids and Madams 41

5   The White Man's Burden 61

6   Diary of a Bored Housewife 78
September 20th, 1978

7   Power Point Presentation *'Ridicularity'* 86

8   Victoria Avenue, Kensington B. 88

9   Different and Differences 105

10   "Oh the Places You'll Go." 124
– Dr. Seuss

11   A Lonely Little Petunia in an Onion Patch 159

12   A White Woman in South Africa 165

13   An Ounce of Gold 175

14	"We can Change South Africa on the Rugby Field"............................ *– Danie Craven, 1938*	184
15	The Story of Kamau	190
16	"You must be on Top of Change or Change will be on Top of You." .... *– Mark Victor Hansen*	199
17	Power Point Presentation *'Post-Apartheidarity'* ..... *As heard on the streets*	215
18	"Animals have Few Rights but they Have Every Right to be Here." .... *– Antony Douglas Williams*	222
19	The Rainbow Nation........................	231
20	Departure	250
21	"I am an African…"	261
	Acknowledgements	270

CHAPTER 1

London, UK

December 1977

When I am at home by myself, I like to have the radio on. I catch snippets of conversation as I move from room to room, making beds, vacuuming, Windolening bathroom mirrors, and disinfecting toilets. It is a means for a busy housewife to update herself on world and local news. The BBC's Breakfast Show with Dave Travis fills the silence in my house much like having coffee at the neighbors. My last port of call is the kitchen doing advance preparation for the evening meal, peeling spuds, cutting vegetables, defrosting meat or fish for the family to sit down to a wholesome dinner. The radio, now plainly audible, intones about Harvey Milk, the first openly gay person elected to public office in California.

I was at the kitchen sink, tap water running, washing runner beans, a cold December day. "A clear blue sky and a high depression" said the weatherman. I heard Philip's key turn the lock in the front door, his footsteps in the hall, and the breath on my neck of my returning spouse, the warmth of his arms around my waist. "How would you like to go to South Africa?" he asked. I was proud of my beans, never having had any sort of green thumb and had surprised myself with homegrown beans of perfection.

"South Africa is rather far from Normandy," I murmured connecting to a brief conversation we had yesterday about this year's summer vacation.
"Yes" he laughed, "It is. Would you like to go there?"
"South Africa," I said, dreamily, "I want to see an elephant."
"Listen," he said, "the Company has asked me to go for four months and I told them I would not go without my wife and family and guess what?"
"What?" I said.
"They agreed."

I turned round to face him, wide-eyed, astonished.

"Are you serious?"
"Deadly serious" he replied.

As with most families, bedtime at our house is a set routine of board games, Connect 4, Twister or Sorry or maybe a new game given for a birthday or Christmas. The children's proverbial favorite was the quiz game, 'Tell Me'; spin the revolving arrow until it stops on an alphabet letter, maybe 'T' and name an animal beginning with 'T' – tortoise or tarantula. Easy, but what if the arrow stopped at 'U', not quite so easy? What if the category chosen was 'countries of the world' and the arrow stopped at 'X'? Somewhere amongst my treasures, I have still that little spinning top. Then there is story time. "Mom, can we read this book," a favorite book being shoved under my nose, *'What Katie Did,' 'The Jungle Book,' 'Charlie and the Chocolate Factory.'* Their all-time forever favorite because it scared the willies out of them, was *'Struwwelpeter.'* Of German origin, we have still an old English version, a 1926 disintegrating edition, its graphic colored illustrations doing nothing to spare a child's sensitivities. Friends, too scared to read Struwwelpeter themselves, advised it would give the children nightmares. Au contraire, the children just lapped it up. Here are two of eight verses from the tale of Harriet who simply could not keep her fingers away from matches:

> "It almost makes me cry to tell
> What foolish Harriet befell.
> Mamma and Nurse went out one day
> And left her all alone at play.
> "And see! Oh! What a dreadful thing!
> The fire has caught her apron string;
> Her apron burns, her arms, her hair;
> She burns all over, everywhere."

And a few lines from the story of Conrad who always sucked his thumb:

> "One day, Mamma said:
> Conrad dear,
> I must go out and leave you here.
> But mind now Conrad what I say,
> Don't suck your thumb while I am away.
> The great tall tailor always comes to little boys that suck their thumbs.

And ere they dream what he's about, he takes his great sharp scissors out,
And cuts their thumbs clean off and then,
You know, they never grow again."

The children in bed, it is our time, time to tell of the day's events at the office and happenings in the home; to discuss local and world events, even politics. We both are opinionated; love to debate, world affairs, politics, sex and religion, the more controversial the better. If it were not for the radio, I fear my contributions would be small. However, tonight was different; we had only one topic in mind – South Africa.

I consider myself an ordinary British housewife from Ealing, a suburb of West London. This is not in any way to disparage the great institution of the British housewife but rather a comment on the British fascination with class structure. In the seventies, Ealing in West London was classified as a posh, middle-class neighborhood. Just why, I think, was because Ealing is a quick twenty-five minute commute by Underground train to Central London. Twenty-five minutes to the renowned Selfridges and to stores that give palpitations to the world's fashion divas, Chanel, Cartier, Tiffany. Twenty-five minutes from the threshold of the seven floors of Hamleys, the finest toy store in the world; twenty-five minutes to enjoy high tea or dine *haute cuisine* at Harrods in Knightsbridge, to test whether the rumor is correct that they do not blink an eyelid if you order an elephant. Twenty-five minutes from London's West End theatres, its seat prices out of reach of the average family but a mecca for tourists. Re-thinking the 'posh' situation, I reckon those who can afford West End shows would likely ride by limousine not the London Underground which kind of puts the can on my theory that quick access by public transport to central London, makes for a posh neighborhood. Yes indeed, Ealing is an uppity area. In England, where you live is as important as how you speak, what you do for a living and who you are.

Philip and I have three children. Philip is an accountant in a multi-national company. In British terms, we are white-collar workers striving to do our best to provide good family values for our kids. I keep a meticulous eye on our monthly financial accounts, careful to produce a family budget with a small surplus. It puzzles me that Philip, the accountant, copes daily with other people's millions but wants nothing to do with our few miserable pounds. I suppose it falls into the category of a 'Busman's Holiday.' What exactly the expression 'a Busman's Holiday' means has long defeated me. That a carpenter is not eager to repair the table in his kitchen or a chef not excited to cook his own dinner, I fully understand, but why a bus driver would not want to drive to a vacation is not clear. In my disconnect, I am reminded of Charles Dickens' comment about Jacob Marley being as 'dead as a doornail' and how much more appropriate it would be to be as 'dead as a coffin nail.'

Our budget allows for a modest annual family vacation to an English seaside resort, perhaps Margate or Blackpool or at one of Butlin's Holiday Camps, a raucous, garish, family friendly vacation that only Brits would enjoy where at seven o'clock a.m. the bedroom tannoy booms, "This is your Butlin's Red Coat calling, wakey, wakey boys and girls, time to rise and shine!", perhaps a rental cottage in North Wales or a little more daring, camping in Normandy, France. Our kids' happiness and their values are centre-field to us. That being said, we design our lives to ensure that we have a life of our own and are not held hostage by our children.

The White Man's Burden

We reckon to remain in our house until the chicks have flown the coop and the nest is empty. Sometimes, we fantasize how our lives would change if Philip became President of his Company with a six-figure salary. A jet to our private island, a yacht tied up at the Isle of Wight, a pied-a-terre in Paris, Bermuda or St. Tropez and our London home, a period terrace townhouse in Canonbury Square. Back in the real world, we are content to remain as we are, a loving family in a suburban row of houses like soldiers on parade, the only difference the street number. Through interconnecting party walls, you can count on hearing your neighbor swearing or humping.

We have one car between us, an Austin Cambridge Station Wagon. Philip takes the car to work. I get to use shanks pony, a British colloquialism for walking on my own two feet. We have one son, aged ten and two daughters, seven and just a year – the last one a late-comer because we do not conceive easily.

School is a half-mile walk each way and I walk it six times a day. The factory where Philip works is twenty minutes' drive by car in the opposite direction to Central London, so based on my theory for an upscale area, it follows his office is not in a posh area. On Fridays, Philip takes my grocery list and comes home with the requested items, usually more than the requested items. Philip does not do things in small measure; he can be counted on buying the largest of everything. The theory, I believe, is in quantitative terms and related to his accounting background, the larger the buy the better the value, a theory that does not always hold good. Through an oversight, we had omitted saucepans from our wedding list and I recall sending Philip on a mission to buy a saucepan to boil eggs. He came home with a catering-sized saucepan that would easily have housed a chicken farm. To be fair, over the years, the extra-large saucepan proved itself invaluable many times as a stockpot for stews or soups.

Christmas was always a big family event, with Philip's parents, two brothers, and their wives, their four children and our extended families. My mother-in-law had hosted Christmas all her married life. The time comes in every family when Grandma hands the reins to a daughter. My mother-in-law had three sons and this year it was my elder sister-in-law hosting for the first time. A festive Santa cloth covered the long dining table set for eighteen, the once a year freshly washed and dried Christmas china, a bottle that once contained a two-masted schooner now filled with decorated pine cones, silver and gold Christmas crackers, flimsy red and green paper hats, fruit punch, laced and unlaced. There too was a twenty-pound golden brown, moist roasted turkey, coated with fresh herbs and oozing juices, Brussel sprouts, perfect crisp roast potatoes, cranberry stuffing and to complete the feast, sherry trifle and Christmas pudding, altogether a feast that would have had Scrooge racing to his senses far earlier. We are a family of traditions, none the more so than at Christmas. The Christmas pudding is doused with brandy, the lights dimmed and the host emerges from the kitchen, pudding held high. Grandpa strikes a match to light the brandy and we all watch mesmerized until the trail of blue flames finally dissipates. Someone at the table has a supply of sixpences which have been strategically placed into the Christmas pudding, one for each child, so noticeable as to be conspicuous and eliminate any chance of an urgent Heimlich maneuver. The children know full-well the sixpences are in the pudding but the knowing never quelled the spontaneous shrieks, "got one." Our gift exchange was traditional too. The gift-giving worked on the principle, the more stupid, dimwitted, useless the gift, the funnier, the cleverer, the more esteemed was the giver. Gifts were given with studied insight into the characteristics of the recipients often regrettably, a laugh at another's expense but all in good fun. Gifts were opened one at a time so all could witness the pooping reindeer, the Dr. Who T-shirt or the guest book for the bathroom, huge hoots as the Christmas wrapping paper dropped away revealing the farcical contents. After my father-in-law passed away, we found in a drawer of his dresser an accumulation of years of inane, impractical, Christmas gifts.

As I sat at the Christmas table, it was difficult not to blurt out the news of our looming transfer to South Africa. In deference to the Christmas spirit and this, oh-so-happy family gathering, we had decided to delay revealing our news until after Christmas.

My mother-in-law would be particularly shocked to hear that her youngest grandchildren, our two older children, would be leaving the private schools for which they had crammed successfully for the highly competitive entrance examinations. All three of my mother-in-law's sons had gone to private schools and by convention, her grandchildren should too. My mother-in-law took pains to explain to me that private schools were not for the rich but for the intelligent. Secretly, I was rather delighted to save a whole term's fees. We were, as the saying goes, 'keeping up with the Jones's, living very close to the mark. Indeed, I might go so far as to say, in the long-term, South Africa saved us from bankruptcy.

Though family and friends were thrilled for us and recognized the worth of the opportunity of four months in South Africa, they were not hesitant to point out the negatives. Were we so enraptured with the prospect of travel to South Africa, that we had lost sight of the risk? Why would we go to a country that supports racism, where everybody sleeps with a gun under their pillow? Through media, they had heard the stuff of crime and violence, the uprisings, bombings and shootings the cries of a country in pain and our family and friends were concerned for our safety.

At complex times, odd theories emerge, the type of stupid hypothesis that fuels racism. A quite eminent scientist in a major London newspaper compared the brains of blacks to whites and wrote that the white brain was larger than the black brain implying white people were more intelligent than black. At the time there was increasing racial tension in the black areas of South-East London, Brixton and Peckham and, for a fleeting moment, it passed my mind that my friends and relatives could be prejudiced. Just as quickly, I dismissed it as impossible.

Before we knew of our transfer to South Africa, much of the information about the troubles there had swept over me as not relevant to my daily life of domesticity, nappies, soothers, PAC meetings and three-mile walks to and from school. Now, all had changed. Suddenly, South Africa was very relevant. I spent many hours going through library microfilm, reading newspaper reports about the Soweto student uprising less than two years before; about how South African students wanted the language of education to be English not Afrikaans as imposed by the National Government; that, indeed, many black teachers did not speak Afrikaans. I learned that schools had closed in support of the Soweto activism, students and teachers rioting in the streets, attacking the police with sticks, rocks, bricks, even schoolbags and that the riots had spread to other townships. The newspapers had been full of a name, Steve Biko, a black student activist brutally beaten and finally shot by police. It seemed that, in using anti-riot police to shoot schoolchildren, the South African government had, unwittingly, shot itself in the foot. The shooting of the children made world headlines and began the start of global focus on the racial policies of South Africa and the diplomatic and economic attempts to destabilize the regime.

I had heard political talk about trade sanctions, how effective they would or would not be. I remember well the request not to buy South African wines. Other than that, life in the UK continued as usual except that while I was going about the family duties of a quiet, suburban British housewife, unknown to me London had become the epicenter of the International under-ground movement opposing Apartheid.

The public condemnation of Apartheid and South Africa's instability saw tourist numbers dropping dramatically. In the seventies, those glossy colored travel brochures were not luring those under gray skies to tropical paradises, pristine white sandy beaches, crystal-clear seas and martinis round the pool. It was still mainly the era of poorly stabilized big ocean liners rounding the rough seas of the Cape of Good Hope, passengers spending much of the voyage seasick below decks. As the airplane industry evolved with fast jet flights, public awareness of Apartheid saw South Africa on the 'No Fly' list, a 'non-U' place to go.

The reports of whites killing black children were scary but I was not going to this country naively, innocent of its issues. I am skeptical on the topic of media bias and sought out the most reliable information I could find. I have to say the venture presented me not only with excitement but with challenge and call. The fact that it was not to be a joy ride hardened my resolve to go. To those I met who expressed concern or criticism, I countered: "Maybe we can make a small difference if we go. For certain, we cannot make any difference if we don't and going does not mean we support Apartheid.

Many Brits still called South Africa home or had relatives living there as did I–my father's two brothers lived in Cape Town. When my Uncle Mac came over to the UK from South Africa to attend my wedding, I briefly touched on the possibility of us immigrating to South Africa. He dismissed my remark with "Over my dead body, it's a time bomb in waiting, not a place for two young people to start a family." Ironically, my uncle never got to know we lived in South Africa. He passed away a year before our temporary transfer there.

Britain had closer ties with South Africa than other countries. South Africa had been a member of the British Commonwealth of Nations, the British Queen its head of state. In 1961, South Africa declared itself a Republic opting out of the British Commonwealth. Nevertheless, there were long-standing ties between Britain and South Africa, an affectionate cousin. It was a delicate political balance; Britain had big commercial assets there. The UK was South Africa's largest foreign investor and South Africa was the UK's third biggest export market. Margaret Thatcher, the then British Prime Minister, openly gave credit to white South Africans for the country's extraordinary economic development and for that she was wrongly labeled as an Apartheid supporter. In fact, Margaret Thatcher was a fierce supporter of human rights as she was of the London underground movement opposing Apartheid. Her reluctance to impose economic sanctions on the country was because of her fear it would bring more poverty to the very people she was trying to help. In the huge political controversy, Philip's English company was prickly at having a branch in South Africa. The reason for his assignment was to close the branch as inconspicuously as possible.

Philip left for South Africa two weeks before us to be Acting CEO of his company's branch in Johannesburg. It was a small unit selling theatre and television lighting as well as mining metrology equipment. Early next morning he telephoned home.

"Jealous of you in the sun," I said. "How's it over there?"
Weird to be speaking to my spouse in South Africa. "Sounds like you're just round the corner." I said.
"Well, yes, it would do because I am just round the corner," replied Philip, "I'm in a hotel at Heathrow. We took off. The plane circled round for an hour and landed again."
"Why didn't you come home?" I asked.
"Well, it was midnight and the flight they have me on is at eight this morning so they put me up overnight at the Delta Hotel which is where I am now."
So much for sunny South Africa!

My British school geography had been about soil types, ridges, rock structures and subcutaneous layers; not about the diversity of countries, their customs and traditions. I was not sure I could even locate South Africa on the kid's globe. We are an insular lot we Brits, if not a lazy lot. Despite its tiny size, the United Kingdom is a major world player. Our Queen is the constitutional head of many countries so we think there is little reason to learn the geography of other countries nor is there any reason to learn other languages since the whole world speaks English!

The White Man's Burden

An absence of four months is not long to lease out a house but we reckoned a furnished house might attract someone temporarily in London. One's home is full of 'stuff' and that is okay when it is just you at home but when it is a stranger moving in, it is a whole different story. I could leave our basic china and cutlery for the tenant. However, the best dinner service, the Royal Doulton with gold-rimmed plates, the dainty rose-patterned tea set inherited from my mom, the cut-glass salad bowl, the crystal sherry glasses, the gold-plated serving spoons, were not for a stranger. It was not for sentimental reasons alone but for practical reasons of damage and insurance. Today, dainty rose-patterned tea cups and saucers and Royal Doulton dinner services are relegated to thrift shops – but those times were yet to come. What to do with the albums of old photos of grandparents, aunts, uncles, long passed, and the photographs of the baby in the bath and the baby out of the bath, what to do with our household bills of interest only to Her Majesty's Inland Revenue. The attic or loft was an away place accessed by a ladder operated on a pulley. I made numerous, sweaty trips up and down that ladder, physically exhausted but energized by excitement at the enormity of our upcoming adventure. My brother's wife was very helpful but the choice of what went up the ladder was mine alone.

It was a terrific opportunity for us as a family to experience a country where without company sponsorship there was no way we would have ever made it on our own. I notified the elite private schools where the children had completed only one year that we would be taking them away for four months. I was so thrilled to be embarking on a four month adventure, living and learning in a country so geographically, culturally, environmentally and climatically different, an education in itself that would fully compensate for the children's absence from British schooling.

The White Man's Burden

The Estate Agent rang with good news. He had found somebody who wanted a short-term rental. We still had one problem, where to leave our pure white cat, 'Kirky.' Further good news, the renter was happy to look after Kirky. His children would love to have a cat.

Things were going well. We were packed, ready and waiting for the taxi to take us to the airport when the telephone rang. It was the Estate Agent. The renter had cried off. Panic! With the front-door keys in my hand, I uttered a few expletives. Then I did a rethink. The world would not end if the house stayed empty for four months. However, it would be a catastrophe to leave the cat in an empty house. Again, we lucked out. The renter who had reneged agreed to take the cat to wherever he was going.

From Heathrow London, to Johannesburg, South Africa, a flight of fourteen hours, was a protracted journey made all the more so by three small children, Philip being already in South Africa. A doctor friend of mine who had himself experienced the nightmare of flying long distance with small children, asked "Did I want something for the kids?" *Wonderful idea, I thought.* He gave me a bottle of clear liquid, three teaspoons for the nine year old, two for the six year old and one for the baby.

I locked the door of the house for the last time for four months. As it turned out, it would be two years not four months, before we would unlock that door again and, even then, only for three weeks.

CHAPTER 2

Arrival

Johannesburg, South Africa
January 19, 1978

Flying through the night, our fourteen-hour flight from Heathrow to Johannesburg was blissfully peaceful. The sleeping-aid taken by the spoonful soon after we boarded was a pre-operative sedative and the kids were out like a light. Had I not nudged them awake, they would have slept through breakfast. As for me, well, when the children are asleep, I crash as a sloth but a sloth with one eye open. Years later, when I related the story to my older daughter, the mother of four small children, she was horrified. She perceived me as being irresponsible. I had DRUGGED my children; the Ministry of Children and Family Services could have whisked them all into foster care!

In 1978, most African states opposed Apartheid and prohibited South African Airways from landing in or flying over any African country. This meant South African Airways had to fly

The White Man's Burden

'round the bulge' of Africa and added considerable extra hours to the flying time. For this reason, we chose to fly British Airways. We stopped for refueling in Nairobi, Kenya. The plane sat on the tarmac for four hours in the heat of the midday sun, engines stopped, air conditioning off, doors thrown wide open to allow air into the cabin – windless, hot, clammy air which did nothing to cool the already hot cabin. Surely it does not take four hours to refuel a plane but it did. On our British Airways flight, there was political fall-out too.

Because there were white South African Nationals on board, no passengers were allowed either to deplane nor even stand at the top of the ramp. The plane's refrigeration system was shut down and strict hygiene regulations were enforced; no drinks or food served. The cabin crew did give me permission to take a pre-made bottle of baby formula out of the fridge. The kids and I were hot, sweaty, frustrated with nothing to do for four hours. It was a total nightmare. In essence, the South Africans on board were holding the passengers hostage. It crossed my mind that some form of retaliation could develop but all remained calm, as calm as is possible with three hundred passengers stuck on a grounded airplane for four hours.

For long family journeys, I usually bring items to amuse the children, drawing paper, coloring books, crayons, pencils for noughts and crosses, hangman or join the dots. However, there is only so much to occupy three rambunctious children long-term in a grounded airplane. After I had run out of steam on word games, boredom set in, tantrums, teasing, pinching, arguments, crying, squealing and screaming. When they were not doing any of these, they raced wildly up and down the aisle throwing paper darts which landed haphazardly around the cabin. The behavior of my kids I thought must be a terrible irritation to the passengers and they were an embarrassment to me. However, the good humor of the passengers surprised me. Hard to believe but it seemed my children's exuberant behavior provided distraction and entertainment for the similarly bored passengers. Many passengers had quite long conversations with the kids and redirected the paper darts with amusement and enthusiasm. Without the sense of fun and forbearance of the passengers, the four-hour touchdown on the tarmac would have been beyond endurance. This is the one time I have been thankful that Old Father Time relentlessly rolls along. It was a huge relief to lift off and eventually resume our flight to Johannesburg.

There is an apocryphal tale of a scene alleged to have taken place on board a British Airways flight between Johannesburg and London.

> "A white South African woman, about 50 years old, was seated next to a black man. Disturbed by this, she called the airhostess. "Madam, what is the matter?" the hostess asked. "You obviously do not see it then?" she responded. "You placed me next to a black man. I do not agree to sit next to someone from such a repugnant group. Give me an alternative seat." "Be calm please," the hostess replied. "Almost all the places on this flight are taken. I will go to see if another place is available." The Hostess went away and then came back a few minutes later. "Madam, just as I thought, there are no other available seats in the economy class. I spoke to the captain and he informed me that there is also no seat in the business class. All the same, we still have one place in the first class." Before the woman

could say anything, the hostess continued, "It is not usual for our company to permit someone from the economy class to sit in the first class. However, given the circumstances, the captain feels that it would be scandalous to make someone sit next to someone so disgusting." She turned to the black man and said, "Therefore, Sir, if you would like to please collect your hand luggage, a seat awaits you in first class." At that moment, the other passengers, who were shocked by what they had just witnessed, stood up and applauded."

A four months' stay, three passengers and a baby, make for a mountain of luggage. Granted, summer clothes take up less room but we had been warned that nights get cool and not to forget the woollies Then, there are those many items that simply cannot be left behind, Big Teddy, 'Tell Me', Barbie and Ken with their extensive wardrobes, bathroom and bedroom not to forget the My Little Ponies, dapple, grey and bay, their brushes and combs, 'the my princess dress' and 'the my ballet dress', the cuddle blanket and the orange tee-shirt with the treble clef motif. Though we had considerable luggage, we were not, as we would be today, taking a folding crib, pack 'n play, booster seat, baby bouncer, baby Bjorn or a car seat which was not the law then in the UK or in South Africa. After landing at Jan Smuts International Airport, it took a full hour to retrieve and collate our eight suitcases and the stroller off the carousel. The kids, again, got into conversations with waiting passengers. *It occurred to me that my children were markedly outgoing – like their mom.*

I reckoned on using two trolleys for the bags. Elizabeth was clinging to my legs, tired and miserable. When the stroller was pulled from the carousel, she adamantly refused to use it and

I had to carry her. The kids were good spotters and Nicholas, at ten, did his best to help his one arm mom grab and haul the heavy bags off the carousel. However, I was hugely thankful to the kindly young man who muscled in on the task. The bags stacked, I sat Elizabeth atop a trolley and, of course, she immediately perked up. On the way to Customs, our bags dropped off the trolleys haphazardly hither and thither, and several times we had to stop to restack the bags. I fancy we must have made a comic sight. At Customs, we were directed to Immigration. A military-type Immigration Officer perused my passport, asked a few questions about destination, length of stay, purpose of visit. As he stood up to hand me my passport, I noticed stamped into a page the name and address of a school, Bryandale Primary School, the school South African authorities designated for the children to attend and in a week's time too. This was my first brush with the system of orderliness and structure I would come to know so well in our South Africa adventure. I also noticed the Immigration Officer was wearing a gun.

On the way to the arrivals exit, we gave another performance of our comedy routine, bags falling wily-nilly off the trolleys.

Waiting at the exit was an eager, suntanned and very overjoyed Philip and it was a reunion with hugs and kisses all-round. The challenge now was how to fit the luggage into Philip's estate wagon. In our frustration, we whispered that one option was to leave the kids behind. I am pretty sure (and hope) this was said up wind, our tired kids out of hearing. My wonderful calm, logical and resourceful husband was fast to resolve the problem and, in minutes, interwoven like pieces of a jigsaw, the suitcases were stowed on the roof-rack, some bags in the trunk and small hand luggage balanced on our laps. Four weary travelers but still fired with excitement, set off on the last leg of our journey to the rented furnished house that was to be our home for the next four months.

The drive from the airport was on four-lane highways past large billboards, factories, office blocks, eighteen wheel rigs, taxis, buses and cars bumper-to bumper made worse by rush-hour traffic. After about thirty minutes, the busy freeway evolved into less congested minor roads as we passed through Johannesburg's suburbs with treed avenues, green verges and residential housing mostly set back behind large trees, gates and high walls. There were familiar English flowers, hollyhocks, snapdragons and foxgloves but they were twice the size and much more vivid. I recognized the massive, bowl-shaped, pointy-leafed protea, the national flower of South Africa and the unmistakable strelitzia, bright orange, yellow and blue, like a bird of paradise in flight. I recognized from African movies, the wide flat-topped acacia tree only this time for real. It was January and mid-summer in Johannesburg.

Philip had made a previous reconnoiter of the outside of the house and knew exactly where to draw up the car. He stopped at a pair of iron gates sided by high white brick walls and draped with hanging pink Bougainvillea. He had signed the paper work with the owner's sister without seeing inside the house so it was the first time inside the house for him as well.

Through the gates, I could see the house was long and low-lying with a sloping tiled roof and green ivy creeping up the walls. In Britain, it would be called a bungalow, in Canada, a ranch bungalow or a one-storey. Pre-empting me to open the front gates appeared a tall, willowy black man in denim overalls. The lease included a live-in maid and a garden boy. I took this to be the garden boy. It was a short drive to the front door of the house. The kids seemed somewhat overwhelmed and held back in the car while Philip untied the bungee straps holding the bags on the roof-rack and I nipped round to unlock the boot to get our suitcases. With astonishing dexterity and grace, the tall black figure that had opened and closed the gates zoomed to the rear of the car, picked up our suitcases three under each arm and two on his head while we, in procession, trooped behind him up the paved pathway to the front door of the house.

Short-term rentals were difficult to find and Philip had little choice but to make concessions. Our preference was four bedrooms and a swimming pool but the concessions he had to make were no swimming pool and three bedrooms. We could have done with that fourth bedroom. We had an older girl and an older boy in addition to a baby. We entered the house to a square white-tiled hall. A cursory look around revealed two rooms either side of the hall, double glass doors one side and a round archway the other. A passageway led off the hall which I thought was probably where the bedrooms lay. Our many suitcases were stacked neatly inside the front door. For certain, the tall figure in overalls had done a better job with the suitcases than we had at the airport. He was about to pick up two suitcases. *Better start off on the right footing, I thought.* "I'm Judy," I said, extending my right hand. No hand came to meet it. "Yes Ma'am, Philemon," said the tall willowy figure disappearing up the passageway. Philemon seemed a man of few words and he was certainly no tour guide.

The older kids were quick to navigate the house. Squeals of delight emanated from the bedrooms as they discovered jigsaw puzzles, boxed games, wooden toys, metal toy cars, books and heaps of soft toys; this house had known children before. Elizabeth crawled to an odd-looking yellow knitted doll with a black hat rather like a Chassidic Rabbi, dreadlocks and all. "Jake" became her inseparable sleeping partner and, thirty-eight years later, I still have him.

As anticipated, the three bedrooms were a problem. Nicholas wanted privacy and was anxious about sharing a room with his seven-year-old sister. We showed him our plan to erect a curtain room-divider, which was not soundproof but would provide an element of physical privacy. Occupying the same space created privacy issues for Karen too. As a leaving gift, Karen had been given a set of toy 'sea monkeys' with instructions to put the sea monkeys into water and feed them daily with a teaspoonful of powder from the envelope enclosed and then to watch. Nicholas, impetuous as ever unable to contain his curiosity to see the sea monkeys grow, emptied the entire contents of the packet into the water. The outcome was the sea monkeys *died*. There then broke out a monumental row with tears, screaming, name-calling and fisticuffs. Living together was hard for them. It was a boy and a girl with three years between them. Constant small fights erupted as one poached from the other, teased or caused disturbance. However, in the end, they learned to have some cooperation. In that confined space, there was no alternative.

Not knowing quite what to do at this point, we wandered into the living room to the right of the tiled hall and allowed ourselves to sink into two very comfy sofas. There was a large fireplace with logs set for lighting, a set of fire irons and a filled scuttle. Either side of the fireplace were shelves stuffed to capacity with books. Our check of the dining room revealed a family-sized oak table and six chairs.

Philip said we should introduce ourselves to the maid, Virginia, who was probably in the kitchen. The kitchen was an old-fashioned country kitchen, looking very functional, with white wooden cupboards, a porcelain sink, and a white tiled floor. In the centre of the kitchen was a rectangular table covered with an oilskin cloth. However, when we entered the kitchen, Virginia was not there.

I was anxious to see if a cot had been provided as promised by the landlord's sister, so we looked at the small bedroom first, relieved to find the lady as good as her word, a cot in place. Of big interest to me was the master bedroom and I was not to be disappointed. The master bedroom was exceptionally elegant with two sets of lead-paned glass windows and a crystal glass central light fixture. There were wall-to-wall floor to ceiling closets with cupboards and drawers, a neat lady's vanity dresser with a pleated skirt in a rose-patterned fabric, so feminine, with three arc-shaped gold-edged adjustable mirrors. To complete the picture, in front of the dresser was a little bench seat upholstered in the same matching fabric. Either side of the queen-sized bed was a nightstand, each bearing a brass table lamp with a flowered lampshade and, on one of the tables, an electric clock. We would be very comfortable in this room. Indeed, we would all be very comfortable in this house.

That first evening at Pytchley Road, Bryanston, I had an odd feeling of being in limbo. I knew no one and was 6,000 miles from home. *Take one-step at a time* I thought, like Neil Armstrong landing on the moon, though to put things in proportion, millions had already landed under this South African moon and now five more!

It was just before 6 p.m. Sunset is sudden in Johannesburg, no gradual sunset, no twilight. It is either light or dark, and darkness had descended. We were going to have to get used to this difference. The kids wanted to see the garden though it was pitch black outside. The lights filtering through the back windows provided just sufficient light for us to make out an expanse of lawn and the outline of a Weeping Willow.

The baby was fussing – no wonder. She needed to eat and to sleep. I had brought jars and bottles and, rather than venture into the unknowns of the kitchen, I fed her in the living room, took her to the bedroom with the cot, ever grateful to our landlord's sister. Head on mattress, poor lamb was out like a light.

We congregated back in the living room to take stock of all we had seen and to think what to do, where to go from here. *Guess, I need to do something about eats, I thought.*

We heard a slight tap on the door, which edged open to reveal two black eyes followed by a comely woman in a short pale-blue buttoned dress, a bandana and an apron. "Make dinner, Ma'am?" It seemed Virginia had decided to take the initiative. I am not often speechless but my tongue got stuck. Maids vanished from British society in the late 1920s and the prospect of having two servants at my beck and call scared me witless. Philip came to the rescue. "Ah, Virginia, would you do that? Thank you so much. We are all hungry." "Yes Master."

The White Man's Burden

A clatter of plates and glasses emanated from the dining room. Virginia, it seemed, was in action. When the living room door opened again, it was Virginia signaling that we should move to the dining room. Travel weary, we were more tired than hungry. At this stage, I was, frankly, beyond caring what was the unknown repast awaiting us. When all was cooked and laid before me, it would brook no argument from me. As we sat down, the aroma in the dining room was enticing. A white tablecloth, white linen napkins, silver cutlery, a jug of water, glasses and two wine glasses were set on the long dining room table. A glass oven-dish and a large china tureen sat on tablemats, slight whiffs of steam escaping both. I took the lid off the glass-oven dish and within was a cottage pie topped with creamed, well-browned potatoes. The china tureen held a yellow mix; we speculated it was pumpkin. The whole thing looked inviting and delicious. Our digestive juices ran and our appetites returned instantaneously. Thus, we ate our first dinner in Bryanston, South Africa.

We did not meet our landlord until we visited Cape Town and there he wined and dined us right royally. He was a Member of Parliament in the opposition party, the Federal Progressive Party; his constituency was Orange Grove near Johannesburg, a cosmopolitan neighborhood of Italian and Jewish whites. At the time, to be in opposition to the National Party, the party of Apartheid, was a formidable challenge. The Progressive Party was openly liberal, termed "leftist," its policy to extend rights to all South Africans.

Every six months, South Africa moved Parliament from Pretoria to Cape Town and then back to Pretoria, the reason given to decentralize and spread power. I heard Opposition Party MPs were not as well remunerated as National Party MPs which may have been the reason he rented out his home when he had to move to Cape Town. I wondered how his children took to the instability of changing schools every six months but likely it was no big deal because they changed to the same school with the same school friends.

The bed linen in all three bedrooms had been turned back, readied for its incumbents and looked very inviting. We dispatched Nicholas and Karen to their curtain-divided bedroom for their first night's sleep in the Republic of South Africa. In a matter of minutes, we also crashed in the sleep of the exhausted, in comfort and bliss.

CHAPTER 3

Settling In

It was that time of early morning when dreams are fading, for me often a time of funny dreams. I have been woken up by the sound of my own laughter wishing desperately to remain in the dream. Sadly, dreams slip away and cannot be resumed.

The rattle of rolling wheels intruded into my returning consciousness and into the beginning of our first morning in South Africa. There it was again, that rattle. The bedroom doorknob turned. No knock, the door simply opened. In rolled a trolley, set with a coffee pot, two cups and saucers, sugar and milk, our early morning wake-up call. I checked the bedside clock. It was 6.00 a.m. Philip was stirring but not fully awake. Virginia left the trolley by my side of the bed. Surprise overtook me and I forgot my manners – no "Good morning, Virginia" or "thank you, Virginia." I nudged Philip.

"You have a cup of coffee."
"What the hell time does she start?"

"What the hell time do you go to work?" I asked, awake, Philip replied tersely, "not this early."

We had experienced the first of what was to become a regular early morning ritual. At 6.00 each morning, Virginia wheeled the trolley set with coffee pot, cups and milk into our bedroom. Our request that she knock before she entered had failed miserably. This was South African lesson 101, 'Embedded Rituals Cannot Be Changed.' It was impossible to anticipate the exact moment the door handle would turn and the trolley roll in. Pre-empting the trolley's arrival was a judgment call, a tricky business. We lay in bed quietly challenging each other to be the first to hear her footsteps or the rattle of the wheels.

"I think she's coming"
"I didn't hear anything"
"Yes, she's here"

This left Philip with two options. He either had to be out of bed and decently clad or remain in bed until after Virginia left. He had to be in the office at 8.30 a.m. which meant battling the morning rush hour traffic and, ideally he should be on the road by 7.45 am. It was always a risky business, a matter of chance – Philip out of bed fully dressed or Philip stuck with one leg in his pajamas!

Year-old babies tend to wake early. Elizabeth would entertain herself playing with her fingers and toes for half an hour but from then on her screams and wails tugged at the heart and jarred on the ears. We would bring her to our bed where she would snuggle down very contentedly between us. The older kids were not reporting for school until next week and this morning, they could sleep in, catch up on jetlag.

The White Man's Burden

School would not start for a week. Newly arrived in South Africa and not knowing a soul there stretched before us a week of empty days. It turned out filling those empty days was not a problem. The garden alone held much that was new to us. It was as though Mother Nature had thrown us a welcome party. The garden was a veritable storehouse of brightly colored birds, strange new flowers, insects, caterpillars, butterflies, dragonflies, lemon bushes and orange trees. The kids were fascinated by the many insects, oversized cockroaches, ugly bugs and huge ants. Bryanston beetles were giant-sized, gross and icky yet in their own way weirdly beautiful. In the garden, they were acceptable but how these creepers got inside the house, I could not fathom. Along our hallways, it was daily routine to step over or walk around big fat, slimy, lazy and immobile slobs. Nobody bothered to move them. Virginia called them by an Afrikaan or Zulu word, which sounded like Khaw-Kwaw. Decades later, our family still refers to all insects as "Khaw-Khaw's."

Nature is its own watering-can. Daily in summer between 4.00 and 4.30 pm, the garden was doused by a torrential tropical storm. It was our indigenous garden watering itself. Assorted ground covers and shrubs with silvery, fuzzy and spiky leaves left no room for weeds and the garden flourished, died, renewed and replenished with no help from us. The red earth of Africa in our garden required nothing more than a twice yearly barrow-load of mulch and fertilizer.

The big Willow tree offered an open invitation to the children to climb its dense and solid branches. At times when I knew they were trying to avoid bedtime or a chore, I knew to look up into the big Willow tree. New to British ex-pats were trees with lemons, short bushy with yellow buds waiting to mature, peaches not fully ripened, still white and green with hairy coats. As we were later to find, the ripened peaches in our garden were deliciously juicy, much sweeter than the peaches in the fruit stores of London.

"We don't see butterflies anymore," was often heard in England. Insecticides and population growth are making for fewer butterflies. Like the canary in the coalmine, the decline of butterflies warns that all is not well in the ecosystem. However, in our South African garden, there seemed no shortage of butterflies, no indication of change although I was told there have been losses of certain species here too. The large orange and black African Monarchs, the Green-banded Swallowtails, the Garden Commodores, the Citrus Swallowdales, and the swarms of white butterflies descended as white clouds on plant leaves only to rise again and flitter away to some other garden. The construction of the butterfly is beyond beauty, like an abstract painting, a Picasso, a Jackson Pollock; butterflies surely, rank among the 'Wonders of the world'. It is perhaps cause for reflection that, though these beautiful fragile creatures have beauty and freedom, it is only fleeting since the life of a butterfly is only in weeks.

At first it was butterfly watching. Then it was butterfly chasing. A net on a pole in the garage, in fact a fish net, served to chase butterflies although it was altogether too large. Nicholas had the idea to pin the butterflies on to a board to decorate the walls of their bedroom. He said that's what lepidopterists do. Thankfully, the butterflies were cleverer and quicker than the children; most evaded the net and those delicate works of art lived to tell another day. The children held numerous insects prisoners in jam jars. I felt a tad sorry for the trapped little guys and would free them when the kids lost interest. A species of insect heard but never seen was the cicada. Each night, there arose a strident cadence of cicadas or was it crickets or was it grasshoppers, in quite deafening songs of courtship which persisted until dawn.

Many birds stopped to say hello and the children and I were so interested in bird spotting that Philip bought a book on South African birds. We thought we had correctly identified a Red Bishop, a fluffy bird, brightly colored with red, orange and black plumage and another frequent visitor, a large bird, the Hoopoe with a metallic green body and a long curved red bill, slightly scary when it swoops to land. By the hundreds like the British common sparrow, were little grey plain birds, the Grey Lourie, oddly dull in this paradise of color.

There was a hammock under the shade of the large willow tree. The lazy, hazy days of summer could have been truly lazy if it were not for the fact I had a crawling baby on the cusp of walking. However, the hammock proved itself a cradle for rocking Elizabeth to sleep, leaving me reading time. Also, in the garden was a swing ball tennis game. A tennis ball on end of a rope attached to a rotating pole was set firmly in the ground. Using tennis racquets, the object of the game was to maintain a volley with the ball on the rope. It was much like tennis but less onerous since the ball could not stray. Nicholas and Karen became competitive, who would make the most hits in one round? I believe the top score was three hundred.

At 4.00 to the minute every afternoon, the tea tray arrived for the Madam. In the summer, it would be set on the patio. A winter mid-afternoon could be nippy and the tea tray would be set in the living room. Should I be out for the afternoon, I would return to find said tea tray in situ and a pot of cold tea, another South African lesson 101, 'Embedded Rituals Cannot Be Changed'!

The package of house, housemaid and garden boy also included two dogs, Alex, an Alsatian (known in Europe as a German Shepard) and Diggory, a Pomeranian. Alex was the guard and yard dog. Diggory was the house pet, a cute, puffed-up fur ball, thoroughly spoiled. Our landlord's sister told us Diggory had a heart murmur and required a daily pill which Virginia had instructions to administer. Relentlessly each day, Virginia and Diggory would perform the ritual chase, Diggory determined not to take the pill and Virginia equally determined to administer the pill. One day, finding the whole process a little irritating, I volunteered to give Diggory his pill. He took it like a lamb, licked it off my hand.

There was a dog leash hanging on a peg in the kitchen. I was feeling confined and thought to get some exercise. With Alex on the leash and Elizabeth in the stroller, I went for a walk to explore the area beyond the main gates. I had walked no further than a few yards when a black man approached me.

"Ma'am", he said, "What do you think you're doing?"
"Just taking a walk", I answered.
"Go home" he said, sternly, pointing a finger towards my garden gate.

The black man was warning me that it was not safe for a white madam to be alone on the streets even with a dog. No more walks for me, for Elizabeth or for Alex. It was a brush with Apartheid somewhat in the reverse way.

The White Man's Burden

Alex, the guard dog, would give his permission to any white man or woman to enter through the main house gates. However, Alex sprang into guard dog mode, baring his teeth and growling when a black man or woman wished to enter. Now dogs cannot be racist and I queried this strange behavior with other dog owners. I got several responses. One was the canine smell mechanism. Dogs have one million times better smell than us. While Alex was familiar with the smell of Virginia and Philomen, he was alert to any new smells. However, this did not explain why Alex was not alert to the new smells of white humans. I learned that Alex was perhaps not socialized as a puppy with black people. I learned that human personal body odor can be changed by diet, the Western diet being different from the black South African diet; that there is perhaps the element of fear of different skin color. I learned the dog can assume the pack leader's fear, in this case the Master or the Madam. I make no claim as to the veracity of any of these bizarre explanations. However, what I do claim is – dogs are not racists.

Bryanston is a residential, dormer suburb north of Johannesburg. If an upscale area is defined by size of house and acreage, top-notch security or by trees so tall they form an arch over the street, then Bryanston was an affluent suburb with a tang of champagne and old money, a place coveted by the rich, not the famous but the well-educated and the professional. In 1978, Bryanston was known familiarly as "The Mink and Manure" suburb.

Five acres was the minimum lot permitted under municipal by-laws for a home owner to have a horse. Most houses on Pytchley Road had five acres. Our house stood on one acre. Having only one acre of land smacked of the poor relation which likely was true.

The White Man's Burden

Our neighbor had a horse in her backyard but confessed doubts as to its legality because she had only three acres.

With no horse and only one acre, I would watch our deprived kids enviously stroking the nose of the illegal horse through the common garden fence.

The five acres that distinguished Bryanston as an upscale suburb paled in the presence of the Bryanston Country Club, founded in 1951 and patronized by all those who idolized golf, fine eating and class privilege. It was rumored that, in the event of the ever-predicted bloody uprising, white South Africans would take refuge in the Bryanston Country Club, it being the last bastion of British Colonialism. The Club had an eighteen-hole golf course, squash courts, a swimming pool and a first class restaurant. The brochure read: 'Bryanston Country Club presents an exciting challenge; birdies are at a premium and hitting the fairways and the greens is an art to be mastered.'

It being summer and school vacation, with no horse, with no swimming pool and no friends, the Bryanston Country Club swimming pool beckoned strongly. However, to be a member of this auspicious and exclusive club was not merely a matter of "You pays your money." It was a matter of showing breeding, lineage, practically peerage to qualify. The major roadblock to membership was the requirement to be sponsored by a current member. Lord Luck came to our rescue in the person of a former C.E.O. of Philip's company who was a member and who sponsored us as temporary members. We spent most afternoons at the Club by the pool. The world and his wife must have had swimming pools in Bryanston because on weekdays, we were the only people there.

Out of nowhere would appear a tall black waiter wearing a fez, a gleaming white shirt, black vest, black pants, a white napkin draped over one arm, "Drinks for the Madam and the children?" he asked. I would order three cokes. It was hard to keep a straight face as this grandiose apparition reappeared, arm aloft, silver tray balanced on the flat of his hand bearing three bottles of Coca Cola and three water glasses. It would not have been different had the tray held a bottle of Veuve Clicquot.

There was one person who did visit the Club's swimming pool on a regular basis, an older lady. I had many interesting conversations with her about South African life and her career in the British Embassy in Pretoria, insofar as it is possible to converse while keeping an eye on a babbling, tottering, one year old. I missed her company when she left to receive a medal from the Queen in London. Her name was Phyllis. We always referred to her as 'Phyllis from the Foreign Office'.

On Sundays, we would make use of the Bryanston Country Club for Movie Nights. We had no television and Movie Night was a big treat for the children. They were pleasant social gatherings with a self-serve buffet and an opportunity to meet others. The movies were advertised as family movies. However, one or two movies were on the cusp for children. Nicholas later recalls movies with nudity! One movie evening it was 'Monsters from the Black Lagoon' during which our seven year old took refuge under the seat. Philip took her home, leaving me with the tough guy who loved every minute of it.

Swimming at the Bryanston Country Club, exploring flora and fauna, coping with our household staff (which is a story for later), shopping at Bryanston Mall for school uniforms and supplies, the week slipped away and the next week the children, resplendent in their brand new uniforms commenced their first term at Bryandale Primary School. It takes guts to be newbies in a class of twenty pupils, a new school system in a new country. I know it must have been tough for them and I was proud of my children's resilience in the transition to Bryandale Primary. They were real troupers in the way they adapted to change. Feedback I heard was the South African kids were fascinated with the posh, plumb in the mouth, British accents of the new kids on the block. Decades later, Nicholas later told me he had found difficulty settling in but, I know, for sure, both children fared better at school in South Africa than they had later at school in Scotland. It was not long before 'best friends' were made and, of course, the London accents dissolved into South African.

South African schools had Standards not Forms as in British primary schools. Nicholas was in Standard 5 and Karen was in Standard 3. At Bryanston Primary School uniforms were blue shirts or blouses, V-necked sweaters with a yellow stripe, short blue dresses, blue shorts or long pants. Rules and regulations were to obsession as per normal. The guidelines of the day were structure, conformity, regularity, neatness and orderliness, making sure as it were, 'the trains ran on time'. On Enrolment, I received a binder of rules and regulations, codes of conduct, performance, honor, respect, study, discipline and expulsion policy, the name of the Headmaster, the teachers, their various Standard numbers. In particular, we were given the name of the Afrikaans teacher, Mrs. Swan, because both kids had to attend compulsory Immigrant Afrikaans classes. I wondered how difficult they would find Afrikaans. Children have an innate ability to soak up languages and I did not hear that it posed difficulty. Also in the package were the start and end dates of all school terms and breaks plus the dates for the many 'name day' holidays. School hours were mornings from 7:50 a.m. to 1:00 p.m., with a break for a snack midpoint; no afternoon school.

The school required pupils to cover their workbooks with brown paper, each workbook labeled with the Standard number, student's name and subject. The opinion expressed by Nicholas was that it was all a waste of time. Some thirty years later, Karen knows exactly where to find her Standard 3 exercise books retained for sentimental reasons.

Nicholas was a doodler which did not sit well with his teachers. I read in pop psychology that round circle doodles signify emotional people and that practical people doodle straight lines. A large doodle is a sign of confidence and a small doodle indicates an introvert. My doodling is relentlessly the same, round circles that easily expand into elephants. I guess my round elephant doodles would put me in the emotional category which does fit. I cannot put Nicholas's doodles into any pop psychology category. His doodles were messy scrawls, meaningless scribble that obliterated the entire page from corner to corner. On his school term report, the teacher commented "Nicholas desecrates his books with relentless monotony!" The South African penchant for rule, order, neatness, tidiness in life required he kept his books in pristine condition. His frustrated teachers repeatedly asked for the workbooks to be recovered. Since I was the one who did the recovering, I reckon I was more frustrated than his teachers. One thought that strikes me is that perhaps, when we doodle, we are bored or stressed.

The White Man's Burden

When doodling was not the modus operandi, a water pistol was. There is generally good reason why decades later an adult remembers the name of his primary school teacher. Either it is because the teacher made an impact as exceptionally good or exceptionally bad or the teacher brings to mind an incident. Nicholas can recall the name of a teacher at Bryandale Primary School, Mr. Coetzee, because of an incident. Below the balcony overlooking the campus, students strolled on their way to class. Nicholas and a friend were on the balcony overlooking the students, each with a water pistol. Their prank was to spray and drench the students below except that the best laid plans of mice and men do not always work out. Among the students strolling below that balcony was the Vice Principal, Mr. Coetzee. The offending boys were yanked off to the Vice Principal's office. One at a time the boys bent at the waist hands spread wide on the Vice Principal's desk, received a spanking from a 'paddle', something like a table tennis bat but longer. The 'paddling' was just a few swipes but its impact left two sore rears. In 1996 the South African Schools Act banned the use of corporal punishment. I wonder would Mr. Coetzee be flattered today if he knew why he is remembered.

The curriculum for morning school was wholly focused on the three Rs, science, geography and history. In the afternoon, teachers coached tennis, rugby, cricket, swimming. Children good at sports could play at provincial level where the game was more intensive. There were the usual obnoxious parents wildly overboard with dreams and ambitions for their kids, screaming sterling advice and scornful critique from the side lines. Where sport was concerned, I admit shamefully I was not one of those eager parents yelling, "go get it," "go, go, go." I disliked endlessly standing on the sidelines, and confess to an oft silent wish the score would bring the season to a speedy end.

The White Man's Burden

As in the UK, South African children pursued a variety of extra-curricular interests, piano, ballet, gymnastics or martial arts. Nicholas had been a Cub Scout and Karen a Brownie in England and they joined scouts and brownies in Bryanston. Arts and sports are skills that offer endless possibilities for the future. That said, children need to be kids with nothing to do but play, pretend, imagine. The free afternoons of South African schooling gave the children opportunity for play, to simply be children. Friends came round to our house or Nicholas and Karen went to friends' houses. In the UK and Canada where school is all day, activities such as music, dancing and gymnastics have to be crammed into the late afternoon, homework written by tired children before dinner or before bed. I have always thought school work better done in the classroom. So often because the child needs help, it is parents or siblings that do the homework. Therefore, the teacher does not get a true picture of the child's learning and capabilities.

In 1978/9 when Nicholas and Karen were at Bryandale Primary School, it was an all-white public school. My children attended for free while black South African parents had to pay for their children's education. With miserable pay rates or unemployment, few black parents could afford school fees and many black children did not attend school. After the dismantling of Apartheid, Bryandale Primary School became a school for both black and white students. Black and white parents pay R12, 000 ($1,150 CAD) a year and there is free tuition for those on low income. It is compulsory for every child, white or black, to attend school until 15.

I am gregarious by nature and, with the children in school I felt the need for company. I was new to the people and the area and decided if the mountain would not come to Mahomet, then Mahomet must go to the mountain. Having learned from my experience as a white Madam walking her dog, I drove my car to visit my neighbors on their three and five-acre estates, ringing the bell at the gates to gain admission. Most Afrikaners are bilingual in English and Afrikaans but I found it difficult to understand an Afrikaner speaking guttural Afrikaans English. I think I got through to them that I was inviting them to morning coffee but I was in no way sure until a goodly number turned up to the invitation from the mad Englishwoman. In fact, the impression I got was they were highly delighted about the whole venture. Coffee mornings became regular but after I left the road, a friend in Bryanston told me the coffee mornings stopped and everybody reverted to status quo.

Next door to us lived a white South African English couple on a three-acre estate, with no illegal horse and no swimming pool but we had in common a toddler. My neighbor was married to a white surgeon working at Baragwaneth Hospital, the only hospital for black Africans in the Johannesburg area. She told me her husband could leave South Africa to work in Australia, Canada or England, anywhere, at a far higher salary but he felt he would be betraying loyalty to his patients, his country and to himself as a healer. The unstable living situation, a country on the brink of civil war, saw professionals emigrating in droves mainly to British Commonwealth countries.

The brain drain was sorely felt by both white and black South Africans. Feelings ran high among white English South Africans who stayed during Apartheid as to whether those who left for other countries were unpatriotic, selfish, leaving a sinking ship or heroes.

CHAPTER 4

About Maids and Madams

"I wake up at 5:30 am because the Madam and the Master like to have me serve them tea in bed in the morning. My room is just beyond the kitchen at the back of the house. There is no water to wash so I use the outside cold water sprinkler and there is an outside toilet. The first thing I do when I wake up is to put on my blue and white button-up uniform, bandana and apron. Then I walk the few steps from my room to the kitchen.

"In the kitchen, I put on the kettle and get the tea-tray ready. Once the Madam and the Master have their tea in bed, I go to the baby who is awake and crying and I take the baby into the Madam. I set light to the gas under the stockpot to cook up the meat and mealy meal for dinner tonight for the houseboy and me. The stockpot simmers all day because it takes that long for the meat and bones to tenderize. Madam complains of the smell. She says it smells right through the house.

The White Man's Burden

"I make breakfast for the older children before they go to school. The boy likes French toast and chocolate milk in the morning. She likes cereal and fruit juice. I give the baby porridge and milk. There is a pot of Kedgeree for the Master and the Madam. The Master goes to work; the Madam goes to the gym leaving the baby with me. I wrap the baby in a blanket on my back while I clean the house. While the Madam is gone, I make her bed, pick up her clothes and shoes from the floor (she is messy, that one) and put everything away.

"Later in the morning, I take the baby to the park close by and she plays there in the sandpit and on the swings. Madam likes us to get out so that she can call her friends and talk of her mother. I have a friend who goes to the same park, so we meet each other. "I worry about my own children so far away in Lesotho. They miss me. My mother, the children's grandmother, takes care of them. My children cry at night because they want me. They should have their mother. My husband works on a farm and does not earn enough. It is not enough for us to live on and for the children's schools which is why I have to leave Lesotho to work for the Madam. I send home as much of my monthly wages as I can.

"When we get back from the park, Madam likes me to make her a salad for her lunch. She won't eat bread because she's on a diet. Only fish and chicken every day, but she is too, too thin. Then I make lunch for the kids. I wrap the baby in my blanket on my back so she can sleep while I do the ironing.

"Around midday, I am given two hours off. Most times, I sleep. At 2.30 pm, I return to the kitchen, put on the kettle,

set a tray with cups and saucers for Madam's tea which, in the summer, is taken at 4.00 pm on the patio, in the winter, in the dining room.

"Each day, I prepare supper. There are many, many maids looking for jobs. If you do not know how to cook, if you do not have a good reference from a Madam you have no chance of a job. I have worked for many Madams and have references.

"For the family's dinner, I make a stew or I cook chicken and vegetables. At 5:30 pm, I set the table in the dining room. The family eats at 6.00 pm. After they have finished, I clear the table and wash up the dishes. The house boy helps me put away the dishes, saucepans and cutlery so the kitchen is clear for next morning. He washes the floors and the cars, polishes the silver, sets logs in the fire place, mows the lawns and cleans the windows. At about 7.00 pm, I return to my room. Sunday is my day off. I go to church in the morning.

"Madam gives me old toys and clothes which I take with me when I go to see my children, Tsotsie and Girlie, in Maseru, Lesotho, about five hundred miles from Johannesburg. It is very expensive to get there. I used to pay a man who regularly trucks maids to the Homelands. Now, I let the man with the truck stay in my room. I get no rent but he drives me for free. My parents are old now and I think the children are too much for them. We are lucky that we have our own house in Maseru but in the winter the roof leaks and the kids get sick because it is always wet. There is water on the floor and our shoes and clothes are wet. It is very cold in our house in the winter.

The White Man's Burden

"I have good kids, but my youngest girl struggles at school. It costs money for her to have extra lessons; money we don't have. I have a good Madam. She gives me paid leave at Christmas, two weeks to go home to my children. I have worked for her for twelve years. My son Tsotsie's wedding was held in her backyard in summer. She said it would be okay for the black guests to come inside to use her down-stairs washroom."

'Grandmas for Africa', the Stephen Lewis distinguished, humanitarian Foundation raises funds for African grandmothers caring for grandchildren orphaned from AIDS. In the 1970s, either AIDS was not endemic, or maybe it was not recognized for what it was, but there were other reasons why grandmothers took care of their grandchildren. The pay of a farm hand in the Homelands was a pittance – if farm work were to be found – but there was good money to be made working in South African mines. The male head of the family had no choice but to leave his Homeland to work in the mines leaving behind his wife and children. There were devoted fathers who remitted money back to their families and there were fathers who evaded this responsibility. In many families, there were multiple fathers which added more complication. The net result was black mothers had no option but to seek work as maids in the suburbs of Johannesburg leaving their children in the care of grandma. It was an appalling situation as the maid's story above relates its effect to decimate the black family unit. My second maid, Rosemary, had four children looked after by her mother in Pietersburg in the Homeland of Lesotho, five hundred miles away. Local work was scant in the barren rural area around Pietersburg. A good part of her meager wages went to her mother in Pietersburg to help the family eat and to pay for her children's schooling.

The White Man's Burden

African Nannies know best

How to be a Madam was wholly new to me. There was no teacher college to show me how to do the Madam thing. During our two-year stay, we had two maids. Virginia was utterly glum though in no way could I fault her work. Rosemary was outgoing, with a quirky sense of humor and equally a great worker. I determined not to let the white Madam's 'power' get to me. I met Madams who were hygiene fanatics, had their maids sterilize the kitchen cutlery daily, sanitize the toilets twice daily, change the bed linen every day, iron towels, sheets, even diapers, weekly forage into those distant parts behind the fridge, under the stove, spring-clean spring, summer and winter. I heard about Madams who were controllers, obsessors, only satisfied when the house was a photo from Ideal Home. It could have been my black employees felt lucky working for a Madam who was easy-going, let them get on with their job, rarely interfered, criticized or directed. On the other hand, it could have been my lack of supervision left Virginia and Rosemary without structure, no clear model for responsibility and confused about whether they were satisfying my expectations. I have never been a fusser over housework, if anything I am slovenly about it. I only house-clean when dust or mess hits me in the face, do a quick tidy before visitors arrive or when I am anticipating the arrival of my mother who runs her finger through a layer of dust on my dining table with her customary pained expression, revealing to the whole wide world her daughter's deficiencies as a housewife.

Having a human being at my beck and call is luxury and I confess one it is easy to get used to. However I could only accept such luxury if wages were equitable to the job, it was a thirty-five hour week, comfortable sleeping quarters with indoor bathroom facilities, paid vacation, legislated rules for sick-pay, hiring and firing. I knew Madams who would brag that their maid was like family while in truth the maid was the invisible nobody in the kitchen, a robot that performed its duties mechanically with unerring efficiency noticed only if a spot appeared on a carpet or bed linen was not changed on Tuesday. Any deviation from perfection and the Madams came down on the robot like a ton of bricks. It salved the Madam's conscience to make liberal talk; she felt among the 'in' set, those who railed against Apartheid.

I hired Rosemary and between us we drew up an unwritten contract. I have never been a boss but I have been a worker which gave me a head-start on Madams whose résumés referenced only macramé and tennis. About her start time, Rosemary said she was an early riser and preferred to start at 6 am. We agreed she would have an hour's break mid-morning, two hours in the afternoon, Thursday nights and all day Sunday off, in total a forty-five hour week – better than Virginia's sixty hour week but still too long. At her job interview, I asked Rosemary to give me a run down on her daily routine and she outlined a very efficient plan. She would daily generally tidy the house, dust furniture, clean kitchen surfaces, weekly do toilets, laundry, vacuum carpets and change the bed linens. She would wash items for the baby as and when necessary. Once a month she would thoroughly clean one room. Twice a year, there would be a thorough cleaning of curtain rails, window ledges, inside cupboards, walls and paint surfaces. I said I would be responsible for the cooking for our family and looking after Elizabeth. I would also clean the refrigerator and the oven. Rosemary insisted on making early morning coffee (which she brought to our room at a much more reasonable hour, 7 am). And, of course, afternoon tea continued to be served daily at 4 pm.

I asked how she felt about looking after the baby soon to be a toddler on those occasions when I could not take her with me. Her eyes lit up. Her face broke into a radiant smile and I knew I had a caring nanny. I asked if she was willing to babysit the odd evening for which she would be paid by the hour. I told her I was not insisting and if she did not want to do evening babysitting, it was okay to say "no." She said "yes."

I felt that Rosemary knew much more than I did about floor cleaners, furniture polishers, washing detergents, laundry folding, ironing and all that is associated with keeping a sparkling home. I let her get on with her daily routine unsupervised unless something went dreadfully wrong. I found my confidence in her confirmed. Rosemary faultlessly, ad infinitum, did a great job.

There was no washing machine or tumble dryer either at Pytchley Road or later at Victoria Street. It was routine for maids to hand-wash the family laundry. Just before we left England, a new invention was setting the hearts of English housewives aflutter, the twin-tub washing machine. Two rubber hoses ran from the kitchen taps to attach to the machine which washed and spun the laundry to damp. For his invention, John Bloom became a billionaire overnight but strangely his empire failed. I know how grateful were the housewives of Britain to be released from the drudgery of hand-washing and I hope somewhere Mr. Bloom is enjoying his money. In sunny South Africa, it continued to be clothes hand-washed and pegged out on the line to dry.

There was no doubt that having live-in help released me to greater freedom. I was able to have a life outside the home knowing that Elizabeth was happy with a good caring nanny. I hate housework with a vengeance. In England, if I could have afforded a 'char lady', an English house cleaner, it would have been top of my list. No housework for two years was utopia. Having Rosemary was an utter blessing.

I was uncertain of the dynamics of the relationship between Maid and Madam and thought it wise to tread lightly. Rosemary was a live-in maid. It is difficult to live with someone on a day-to-day basis and not to feel at least some sense of tie. There were Madams who developed strong bonds with their maids and the maid felt genuine affection for her white employer, sisterly comfort. There was a possibility I would come to know Rosemary and Virginia well but the unknown was how well they wanted to know me. I am an outgoing type and meeting frequently in the kitchen, living room and bedrooms, I would find it difficult not to make conversation. I was tempted to ask them questions about their lives, their loves, their ambitions, their dreams. Rosemary was cheerful, polite and willing but her disinterest in intimate conversation made it patently clear she saw me as a white woman withal and her 'baas' to boot. I was not a member of her family nor she mine and I should remember that. For the safety of convention, I had to contain my curiosity.

We knew the fifty rand a month in wages we paid to Virginia would not meet a week's food for our family. Her wage was appallingly low. However, we were in a predicament. Virginia was not our maid; she was permanently employed by our landlord though during the time she worked for us, we paid her wages. We would have liked to raise her wages to equal value for service but common sense held us back. When our landlord returned from Cape Town, he may not appreciate paying higher wages and, for sure, Virginia, would not appreciate scaling back to lower wages. The same went for Rosemary. After we left for England, she would have to settle for a new job at the wage level current at the time. We conceded it was best to leave both their wages at status quo. Where we could, we made payments in kind, sick leave, vacation time, time to see her family. She had access to a nutritious and balanced diet, fruit, oranges, bananas, grapes, milk, cheese, eggs, bread, good quality meat, squash, pumpkin, potatoes, salad, freedom to take items from the fridge, gifts at Christmas and for her birthday, items of clothing, makeup, towels, shoes, paid babysitting and extra cash for services provided outside her designated duties such as pool duty, showing me how to weave macramé or knit. I also told her to use the inside toilet although I never saw her do so. I bought a radio for the kitchen and I do know she listened to it.

Each morning I came down to the kitchen to the sickly smell of cooking meat. The pot on the stove simmered all day until Virginia and Philemon ate around 7 pm. We knew nothing of the diet of South African staff and Philip had taken care to ask the landlord's sister at the time of renting about the staff food arrangements, what they ate, cooking, etc. She said they cooked for themselves and to buy 'staff meat' from the butcher in the village. I visited the butcher and saw the item termed 'staff meat'. It was a collection of gristly meatless bones. I was appalled. There was no way I could feed this to any human being and I determined from that moment that staff in my home would feed on good quality meat, beef, lamb, pork or chicken, just as we did.

I thought about the content of our meals and figured if Virginia and Philemon ate Western style it would put an end to the sickly smell in the kitchen from forever boiling meat bones and save gas at the same time. I asked, "Virginia, how about you having your dinner as we do, you know, our meat, our vegetables and potatoes?" She would have good quality meat or fish, fresh vegetables, rice, potatoes and fruit or milk desert. Virginia shook her head, vehemently, and replied, "Like my own food best, Ma'am." I asked Rosemary if she would like to eat the Western way and she said, "No Ma'am, I cook for myself." One can only offer! However, I am certain while in our employ they must have noticed it was not 'staff meat' but lean beef, lamb and pork. Trivial as quality of meat might sound, it represented to me a footprint of caring in South Africa, which would not have happened had we not accepted our assignment.

I did not want to return to England with two spoilt brats. We made a strict rule that the children make their own beds and after meals take the dishes to the kitchen sink. We insisted they be respectful and polite when talking to the domestic staff with always a please and thank you. We would remind the children they were here temporarily; that this artificial way of life was coming to an end and coming soon. I wanted them to understand that it was Virginia's and Rosemary's job to help me with the running of the house but not to do everything for me; that there was much that I did myself around the house in addition to cooking meals, caring for both of them and Elizabeth; and that there was much they could do for themselves such as keeping their rooms tidy, wiping up spills, putting their laundry in the baskets. We discussed that when they saw Rosemary or Philemon carrying groceries or laundry, they should ask if they could help.

The system of Apartheid in South Africa would have an effect on the thinking and behavior of my children. Somehow I had to explain Apartheid to them, its inhumanity, its injustice, its wrongfulness. In their all-white school, there was risk they could be indoctrinated to believe black South Africans were inferior, their place to be always a maid or garden boy. They could become accepting of the situation without question. I felt it was my responsibility to generate discussion and answer questions, which if not asked, I had to raise. Thus, we had many talks about how hard it was to be black in South Africa, why there were no black pupils in their school, how Rosemary had four children whom she loved dearly but had to leave five hundred miles away in order to find work and money to pay for their food and schooling, why black parents paid for school and white parents did not and the indignity of Rosemary's tiny, concrete room, outside toilet and cold shower. I reversed the situation to prove a point and asked the children if, because they had white skin how would they feel if they were banned from swimming pools or beaches and, similarly, were unable to see a movie in a theatre, sit on any seat in the park. It was important for them to understand the wrongfulness of Apartheid and to see our maid and garden boy as human beings who felt the same pain as white people, had the same hopes, the same dreams and aspirations; that black people were parents, uncles, aunts, cousins, sons and daughters who loved and were loved. I firmly believe they had a good grasp of what racial discrimination is and that they did not like it. It was a touchy and delicate balance because I could not risk my children becoming so upset or angry they might openly express their views with friends, even best friends or other adults. Yet, I had to make them understand that Apartheid was wrong; that black people serving the every whim of white people is not how it is in other countries, that in other countries, black people go to school, work in professions and trades, live in houses with modern conveniences and are respected. They were living in a country where it was dangerous to be outspoken, where activism could lead to public reprimand as a dissenter or terrorist. We had to caution them to be careful; that how we felt about Apartheid was not to be discussed outside of our front door, not with their best friends or anybody.

Ever lurking in my mind was the thought that I was enabling the racial regime by taking advantage of underpaid labor; that it was far from my ideal of respect and equality. I soothed myself with a mantra – if it were not for me, two black South Africans would have no job; if it was not for me two black South Africans would be eating fat and bones; if it were not for me four unknown children would be starving in Pietersburg; if it were not for me four children would not go to school. It was a far cry from my ideals for Rosemary, Virginia and their families but it was the reality of the time and I was powerless to do more. Repeating the mantra did nothing to salve my conscience.

We made a practice of getting away from Johannesburg on weekends, particularly weekends attached to a statutory holiday. When we were absent on these long weekends, I always offered opportunity to Rosemary in Kensington B or Virginia in Bryanston, to take time off. Several times I suggested to Virginia she might like to visit her children cared for by her mother five hundred miles away in her Homeland. The boyfriend who shared Virginia's room ran a business ferrying black maids to the Homelands, his deal in exchange for no rent, was to give Virginia a free ride to her Homeland. Her reply surprised me.

"No, Ma'am, I wish to stay here."
"Surely, you want to see your children?" I asked.
"No, Ma'am is better here."

It seemed motherhood was not Virginia's cup of tea; she preferred to be in Johannesburg among her social network.

However, Virginia was not typical of African mothers. Mothering is innate to black South African women. Rosemary was so very happy to be given time off to visit her children. One weekend when we were away, I gave Rosemary a camera to photograph her children, her mother, the children's grandmother at their house halfway between Pretoria and the Zimbabwean border, a rural area not far from Pietersburg in Lesotho. I also well remember being thoroughly chastised by Rosemary for my unmotherly carelessness. Our Victoria Street home had a small but beautiful pool surrounded by large granite rocks and tropical vegetation. The pool was entered through an arched wooden door which did not lock but latched. Elizabeth had wandered off as she was prone to do. Rosemary noticed her missing. She found her in the swimming pool area. The blast of Rosemary's ire, the wagging finger, the scathing admonishment delivered to me about my irresponsible behavior leaving the pool door unlatched, is forever an invisible scar on my forehead.

The White Man's Burden

In white South African culture, the Master of the house did not intervene in the relationship between his wife and the black domestic. The white Madam wielded the power where the maid was concerned. Where the garden boy was concerned, the Master had the say. Maids were often double-duty maid and nanny.

Groups of nannies regularly gathered in the park. The black nannies were a community to themselves. Nanny friends would assemble with their baby charges to sit on the green grass their backs against a wooden bench inscribed, 'Net Blankes' – 'Whites Only'. In the carriage was a pale white baby with blonde hair and clear blue eyes. The other nannies had similar babies. This is Apartheid South Africa and these are the African 'mothers' of white babies. Domestic workers were deemed suitable to bring up their employers' young children, everything from bathing to feeding, babysitting, changing nappies and more, but not decent enough to share life under the same roof, eat off the same plates, sit on the same toilet, eat the same food or sit on the same chairs as their 'superior' white employers. So often were white mothers out to lunch with friends, playing tennis or shopping in the malls, their children came to see the black nanny as their mother.

At Victoria Street when Rosemary babysat in the evenings, we would return home to find her in the living room sitting on the floor. I told her it was perfectly okay with us if she sat on the sofa or an armchair. No matter how many times I told her, we continually arrived home to find her sitting on the floor. I can only conjecture that sitting on the floor was a traditional custom or that it may have reflected a form of inferiority complex engendered by the Apartheid system of racial superiority.

The White Man's Burden

The room in the yard behind the kitchen was the wall between black and white cultures. I had only seen Virginia's room from the outside. What I could see was small, dark and dreary. The maid's room seemed a 'verboten' place, a divide which made it difficult to have any real opportunity to get to know either maid or houseboy. It was not that I did not try. Many times, I would start a conversation only to receive a two-syllable reply – "Yes Ma'am," "No Ma'am." I wondered if hatred for whites fueled their reticence to communicate; if it was a deliberate act of defiance to Apartheid, a self-imposed discipline using silence as a weapon of resistance to avenge the differences in lifestyles or whether we, the white people, had so robbed the black South African of identity, he or she was inherently unable to communicate with whites. At times of inter-communication, the servile existence of their lives was never more apparent.

To my shame, I am horrified to admit that I caught my children amusing themselves at Virginia's expense. They had climbed on the roof of the house and as she crossed the yard from the kitchen to her room, were rolling lemons picked from the lemon trees in the garden, down the roof aimed to fall on her head. Thankfully, they were not good shots and missed their target but we did act quickly to put a stop to it using discipline and restorative justice to right the wrong.

I got myself an 'Afro' hairdo. The 'Afro' haircut, with its tightly permed curls, was the hairstyle trend of that year. When I returned home, gal to gal, I swizzled round in the kitchen to display my new haircut to Rosemary, asking "Do you like it?" "No Ma'am," was the very curt reply. I should have remembered that, while I was trying to curl my hair, black Africans were going to inordinate lengths to straighten their nappy hair with curling irons and hot stones – my new, trendy hairstyle went down like a ton of bricks!!

A houseboy or garden-boy was no boy. All black men were called "boy." Our "boy" was a man in his forties. "Tell the boy to bring round the car," "Ask the boy to light the fire." The "boy" also washed the dishes, polished shoes, mended fuses, moved the freezer, lit the log fire, swept the driveway, mowed the lawns, washed windows, replaced light bulbs, opened and closed the main gates. When I returned from town with groceries, Philemon knew exactly which cupboard, which shelf, which drawer to put each item. I never had a problem finding a jar or a packet. In winter, at 6 pm, he would appear in the living room carrying two logs one under each arm and two abreast – none on his head! "Fire, Ma'am?" he asked. He would kneel down before the fireplace, remove the fireguard, stack the logs on the hearth, and poke the previously set kindling. Drawing from a box of matches in his pocket, he would light the kindling; sit back on his haunches to wait for the kindling to catch. Then he would carefully place a couple of logs one on top of the other, nudging them into position, finally balancing the remaining logs. There was an edge to the autumn night air and a fire was very welcome. One of us would always say, "Thank you, Philemon." There was never a reply. He left, a tall man short on words.

Most of his workday was in the garden. Quite what he did in the garden was not clear. The lawn needed no watering; the climate was its own gardener with a mixture of extreme sun and a daily tropical storm to keep the weeds at bay, the grass grew only to a modest length. There was a quite large square of virgin earth presumably planned to be a vegetable garden but as far as I could see, it contained nothing but a few pumpkins laying as they do, in chain-link formation. He did wash the Master's car on weekends and weekly polished all our shoes. Mostly, I would see Philemon, in his own little world whiling away time under the sun, having a smoke, sucking a reed. A delightful job had Philemon had he a decent bed, an indoor toilet and a warm water shower.

To work in the Transvaal, Rosemary and Virginia had to have the proper papers, the notorious 'pass.' There were conditions to fulfill to get a pass, a 'dompas,' and it had to be carried everywhere at all times. A dompas contained the holder's finger-prints, photograph, place of employment, permission from the Government to be in that part of the country, even employer's reports on worker performance and behavior. Rosemary could only get a pass to leave her Homeland of Lesotho if she had a steady job. If she was out of her Homeland with no pass, it implied she had no job and she would be deported back to the Homeland. Each month, employers were required to stamp the pass to validate employment. We never did because we did not know about it. Many employers overlooked the pass situation insofar as the details were concerned. It was a Catch 22 situation.

Education for blacks was meager, designed to keep them in subordinate roles, to keep them from moving on to further learning and so to retain them as farm laborers, miners and domestic staff. Science, history, geography were not on the curriculum. Arithmetic (as distinct from mathematics) and practical applications such as sewing, cooking, carpentry were. Very few black South Africans made it above Standard 5 or to secondary education, most left school at eleven. There was a small black middle class mainly convenience store owners, cabdrivers, policemen. A very few made it through to college or university but had to be extraordinarily bright, determined and focused.

> *"There is no place for the Bantu in the European community above the level of certain forms of labour. What is the use of teaching the Bantu child mathematics when it cannot use it in practice?"*

Dr. H. F. Verwoerd, then Minister of Native Affairs, later Prime Minister.

I found maids and garden boys were a hot topic in Johannesburg. Madams never tired of talking about maids and garden boys much like Brits talk about the weather. The weather in the Transvaal was consistently perfect so really there was nothing much to say about the weather, but of maids and garden boys, conversation could never be exhausted.

"How's your new maid?"
"Eish, lazy so and so; she's not going to last, this one."
"My maid is on the phone too much; agh, she has more friends than I do; what to do?"

If you wanted to get to know someone, just mention your maid and you would find yourself invited to afternoon tea.

When Virginia was sick, black neighborhood maids walked down the path to her room in droves. I wondered what they talked about. Did she tell them about my wild, precocious kids? What did they say about the odd British family who would soon vanish to another country? How did this English white Madam stack up against her past employers? Did she moan about my inadequacies as a Madam, my pushiness to know things about her life, my attempts to change her diet, did she even have a concept of job satisfaction; did she find repeating the same tasks day after day monotonous drudgery, going nowhere, goal-less? Did a woman with no more than a Standard 5 education, if a Standard 5 education, converse in political terms about inequality and racialism – about Apartheid? *Could she find anything positive to say,* I wondered.

It is interesting to reflect that 19th Century Victorian England, too, was a time of Masters, Madams and domestic workers. A British housemaid was on the lowest rung of society. In Victorian England, it was not racism which created the divide but class distinction. Surprisingly, divisions of class are still intrinsic to Britain. In Victorian England, there was no social safety net to catch if you lost your job, no union to protect you if employers took it on themselves to dismiss you. There was abject poverty in the working class, if you did not earn a living you starved. Those who worked for a British Madam or Lady considered themselves lucky to have a roof over their head, food, a bed and an outhouse.

The White Man's Burden

DAY BY DAY   **by Abe Berry**

Domestic service in Victorian England as in 1970s South Africa was the largest source of employment for women. Wages were abysmal but all-found, food, heat, a room, an inside toilet, made it tolerable. In Britain, a middle class family might employ one housemaid while an upper class family or an aristocratic family would have a whole hierarchy of domestic staff from butler to housekeeper, cook, my lady's maid, the master's valet, footmen, parlor maid, scullery maid, stable groom and gardeners. There was little other work for working class women. The downstairs servants did not mix with the upstairs family. The upstairs toilet was out of bounds for house staff and, while it was not "Baas," it was "Sir" or "Madam." The comparison of racism and class distinction both smack of human superiority. However, those 'below stairs' in Victorian times were poor but they were not seen by their employers as repulsive or brainless. The First World War was the 'Mandela' for change, not because of one-man's leadership, but because of an absurd World War where, when the men went to fight, the women took their place in industry and proved their capabilities in positions other than domestic service.

Near the end of the First World War on July 18th, 1918, a baby boy of Royal birth was born in South Africa.

CHAPTER 5

The White Man's Burden

All was quiet in the house, kids blissfully asleep, mom and dad too, after a frenetic day with three hyperactive children. Nature's chemical agent did its best to replenish our depleted energies but sleep was fragile to me after years of "Mom, I want a drink of water," "Mom, I had a bad dream." My maternal brain was ever alert to any sound that was not the gentle snoring of my spouse or the rustling of the sheets from his restless leg syndrome. A sound evocative of morning penetrated my brain – surely not a dream. There was no reason to interrupt my adventures in the land of Nod but, slowly, I felt the awakening of my wits, my limbs stirring and my arousal to the day that lay ahead. Then I heard it again, a knocking noise. Let it go, my body said; sleep on. The sound was now a clearly audible knocking and the owl in me began to blink. Something was going on and I needed to find out what it was. Fully awake, I nudged Philip, my spouse with the restless leg syndrome.

"Philip, you need to wake up." Philip sleeps as in a coma and, when disturbed, semi-wakes, a zombie, befuddled, disoriented. "Listen, listen," I said. The noise continued as if someone was trying to break a door down. Finally, he murmured, "Yes, I hear it."

In an instant, he was up, the action superman I knew and loved, wielding aloft a brass candlestick edging towards the source of the noise. Timidly, I tiptoed behind. The banging was coming from the kitchen back door and seemed to be the plea of someone frantic to enter. At night, we locked all doors. Most people, wherever they are, lock doors at night but in 1978 South Africa under Apartheid racial laws, white people double-locked doors. We looked at each other questioningly. Was it safe to open the door? Who was it? Why was someone hammering on our kitchen back door at two o'clock in the morning?

We briefly discussed calling the Police. It would involve so much more than we were ready for and was it really necessary? A burglar would have to be real stupid to make such an obvious racket. We turned on the kitchen light and decided to chance opening the door. Like a bat out of hell in rushed our very distraught maid, Virginia. Philip and I exchanged what-to-do-now looks. It seemed best to try to calm her down with some "there, there's" and a "what's wrong?" Attempts to calm her made zero impression on the heaving mound of flesh that collapsed on a kitchen chair, shoulders shaking, emitting loud and penetrating sobs. My first thought, I must admit, was, *I hope this doesn't wake the children.* Despite all our efforts, we could not extract one word from Virginia to explain her plight. We were two tired parents craving sleep and what were we to do with this bawling woman who would

The White Man's Burden

not talk? In desperation, I thought of the British solution – and quickly made a nice cup of tea. Two world wars had been won over a cup of tea. It did the trick. Virginia's sobbing subsided as she drank her tea. Calm but teary, she still refused to talk and Philip and I ushered, if not pushed her, out of the back door to her room off the yard. Well, that was it, all over whatever it was. We locked the back door and collapsed into our now cold, not very welcoming bed, to resume our night's slumber.

I did not fall asleep. I lay there staring into the dark. Philip's irregular breathing assured me he had crossed the threshold. I am not sure how long it was that I lay awake before the banging on the back door started again. I nudged Philip and he woke up, rather quicker this time.

"What shall we do?"
"Hospital" said Philip. "She's off her head."

I thought about the distraught Virginia. Maybe she was ill and calling an ambulance was for the best. I dialed 999.

"Police, Fire, Ambulance, which do you require?"
"Ambulance, please."
"What color blankets?"

What color blankets? Puzzled by the question, I asked the operator to repeat it.

"What color blankets?" he repeated.
"I need an ambulance for my sick maid not blankets."

At this point, I believe the operator clued into the situation, reckoned these were white folks who had not called an ambulance before.

The White Man's Burden

"Black maid, blue blankets; blue ambulance" he said.

Then I understood the relevance of the color and the blankets. Blue blankets were for blacks and would take Virginia to Baragwaneth, the only hospital for blacks in the Johannesburg area. We were meeting Apartheid head-on.

"The color of the blankets?" said Philip, "Can it get worse?"

An ambulance drew up to our gated entrance. In pitch dark, two burly black attendants strode the pathway to the kitchen. The same two black attendants escorted or it would be more accurate to say, pushed a wildly deranged Virginia from the kitchen to the ambulance. The hullabaloo had awakened the older kids who were peering out of the kitchen window thoroughly enjoying the commotion. After Virginia departed for the hospital, we discussed the probability that alcohol was likely responsible for her extraordinary behavior.

How long Virginia would be away I had no idea. Two months earlier I had been an English housewife doing my own housework and cooking for my own family. A maid was not a thought in my head. Not having a maid now was not a big deal. However, now I was a Madam with a maid but not a maid.

To my utter astonishment, twenty-four hours later, Virginia entered the kitchen as if nothing had happened. When she returned, we anticipated she would be reasonably well but in truth she seemed to be far worse than when she left. In the pitch dark of the early morning when she left in the ambulance, we had not been able to see her clearly and boyfriend assault had not entered our heads. Now, in the mid-afternoon, we could see the stitches and bandages, a face battered, bruised and swollen, a puffed-up ball of flesh, eyes sunken to slits.

"Whatever happened, Virginia?"
"Oh Ma'am, I walked into a glass door," a palpable lie.

We were to find out Virginia shared her room off the yard of our house with a man friend from Lesotho. If the Bantu Police had gotten wind of the sharing, the law would have come down heavily not only on her but on us as her landlords. At the time we were unaware of both the man and the law.

Unemployment among domestics was rampant and work ethics with maids very strong for fear of losing their jobs. Despite her horrendous ordeal, Virginia was ready and willing to resume work immediately. Her face was a disaster and I could not imagine the pain she was in. My heart went out to her. Male violence crosses barriers in every country. In South African tribal culture a woman's body was an intrinsic male right; in 1978 black South Africa, a beating from the boyfriend or spouse no big deal. After Apartheid, legislation was introduced that no longer sees domestic violence as a family tiff but, for what it is, a crime. However, relationship abuse still hides itself in the guise of tribal culture. Even in Western society, the victim is still regarded with suspicion and sex a man's right. There is a way to go yet.

I knew it was time to be cruel to be kind for she would fight me to the last to keep at work. "Virginia, "I said, compassionately but emphatically, "I do not want to see you again until your face is healed." She was off for ten days while the healing took place. We watched as a continual parade of maids and garden boys trooped

The White Man's Burden

down the garden path to visit her bearing gifts of chickens, soups, casseroles and fruit. In times of need, the black community is solid in support and friendship. If the boyfriend continued to live with Virginia, we never knew. The maid's room is sacrosanct and squatters go unnoticed. However, we saw no evidence of further physical abuse.

Extract from the Cape Times, May 31, 1969

"Ambulances of the Cape Peninsula Local Authority serving the entire area between Klipheuwel, Elsie's River and Cape Point are not run on an Apartheid basis. When a single ambulance must serve people of different races, the patients are asked – if they are conscious – whether they mind travelling together in the same vehicle."

A flea can trouble a lion more than a lion can trouble a flea.

AFRICAN PROVERB

It was Thursday in Victoria Street. Rosemary was subdued and seemed to be lacking her usual energy.

"Everything okay?"
"Yes Ma'am."

I thought no more of it until Friday morning when she appeared more lethargic than ever. I asked again,

"Rosemary, are you feeling okay?"
"Ma'am, I have a pain."
"Oh," I said, beginning to clue in. "Where is the pain?"
"My mouth, Ma'am, but it will go away, don't worry."

Staring before me were gaps of missing and misaligned front teeth

"Is it a tooth?" I asked.
"Maybe, Ma'am but it is nothing."

She went off to bring in the dry laundry off the garden line, Elizabeth enveloped in a blanket on her back. I was in the kitchen looking at our food stores. We were having people to a Braai (BBQ) on Sunday and I was wondering if we had enough steaks in the freezer and if we needed more snack items, chips, dips, pickles. I glanced at Rosemary who was methodically and neatly folding each laundry item, a process intriguing to watch, corner to corner, crease to crease, the end product as if still in the original store packaging. What I saw then was not the folded clothes but her cheek, red and swollen. I went up to her and turned her round. Yes, the right cheek was twice the size of the left cheek.

"How is the pain?" I asked.
"Not good, Ma'am, but it will go."

I did a quick think. It was Friday. The dentist at Sloane Square Mall did not work Saturdays and Sundays. If things blew up worse, we could end up going to Baragwaneth Hospital for emergency treatment and having to wait hours if not days.

The White Man's Burden

"Rosemary, we're going to the dentist," I told her, "Now," an order, not a request.

"Yes Ma'am."

With the baby on Rosemary's lap, I drove to the dentist. I had taken the children there for check-ups and had, myself, a cavity filled there. Posted on the door at the dentist's office was the ubiquitous list of notices, rules and regulations (one becomes impervious to them). However, that day I had to obey one rule, 'Slegs Blankes' – 'Whites Only'. Outside the dentist's door was a sign 'Blacks Boontoe' with an arrow pointing upstairs, another confrontation with front and center Apartheid. Rosemary went up the back stairs and I went in the ground floor front entrance.

At the reception desk, I explained that Rosemary, my maid, had gone upstairs with a violent toothache and how did I go about coordinating payment. The receptionist gave me an odd stare. Obviously, I had asked a dumb question. "Naturally Madam will pay for her maid's treatment" she said. "The bill will be mailed to you." I enquired of the receptionist if she had any idea how long Rosemary would be. She replied probably about an hour and suggested I might like to do some shopping and come back. An hour would give me time to pick up some bits for the weekend braai and I would then return for Rosemary.

Back at the dentist, it crossed my mind to go up the blacks' stairs. If I flouted this rule, I could really upset the apple cart and I thought better of it. It was asking for trouble. I asked the receptionist if she knew whether Rosemary was finished and she buzzed upstairs to be told Rosemary had a wisdom tooth extracted and had left. She suggested she was probably waiting for me outside. At the roadside, I looked for Rosemary. The streets seemed to be pretty well deserted. I went round a couple of corners but no Rosemary. Shortly, a black boy came up to me.

> "Are you looking for a girl in a short red skirt?"
> "Yes, that's right, she's just had dental work and I'm here to bring her home."
> "Sorry Ma'am, she got picked up just minutes ago by the Bantu Police. She had no pass."

My heart took a lurch. Of course, we had left in a hurry and Rosemary had not had time to bring the purse that contained her pass. All black people had to carry a pass. If they did not carry a pass, they were 'unemployed.' If they were unemployed, the Bantu Police would pick them up just as they had today. The emotional reactions to the pass, this hated piece of bureaucracy, have been compared to the yellow stars Jews were forced to wear in Nazi Germany. The young man seemed concerned and continued:

> "She's probably at the Police Station now. Tomorrow, she will appear in Court in Pretoria. You could catch her there."

I thanked him and went home thinking tomorrow I would have to make the long journey to Pretoria. Philip was away on business. Philip is always away when needed, goes without saying. If he had been home, I could have left the baby with him while I went to Pretoria or he could have gone to Pretoria. My next thought was about Rosemary. She had a wisdom tooth extraction, which can be very painful afterwards. The least I could do was take Tylenol to the Police Station. I gave Elizabeth her supper, picked up the Tylenol from the bathroom cabinet and, with a very crabby baby in tow, took off for the Police Station. There, a sergeant behind the desk asked what I wanted.

> "My maid, Rosemary, is here. She had a tooth extraction and must be in quite some pain. I wonder would you be good enough to give her this Tylenol."
> "Ma'am" the police officer replied irritably, "we picked up 400 maids today." He took the Tylenol.

No maid, no husband, great, I thought, *I would have to bring Elizabeth to Pretoria with me next day.* I walked into an empty house; the kids were at a play-date. A short, buxom figure in a red skirt flung herself at me in a great big bear hug. It was Rosemary. I was in shock.

> "Oh, Ma'am," she said, "It was so awful there – so many people, nobody could sit down, no food."
> "How did you get out?"
> "My uncle," replied Rosemary "Is a policeman."

All over the world, they say it is not what you know but who you know that is important; that is the way the world works. Influence counts even in Apartheid South Africa.

Visits to medical clinics or dentists were few for blackservants, if any, and only if the Madam was prepared to pay the bill. When a black man or woman smiled, the poor health of their mouth was distressingly obvious, gaps of missing, twisted and decaying teeth. The home remedy for sore mouths was vinegar and for burns and infections, it was urine.

The White Man's Burden

The old woman looks after the child to grow its teeth and the young one, in turn, looks after the old woman when she loses her teeth.

AFRICAN PROVERB

One summer's day at Pytchley, I saw a strange man out in the garden. What was he doing there? Virginia came running into the kitchen looking scared.

"Virginia, what's up, do you know that man?"
"Yes, Ma'am, he's after me."
"After you?" I said, "What for?"
"Oh, Ma'am, I do not want to say."

Through the window, I could see a short man with a cap. He was leaning against the doorpost of Virginia's room.

"Well, I don't think he's going away," I said. "Look he's out-side your door. Maybe you should go see what he wants."
"Ma'am, I can't," replied Virginia. Her hands had gone to her face and she was cringing.
"Virginia, you had best tell me what this is all about."
"Ma'am, I am in trouble."
"Well, let me hear about this trouble."
"It's my wig, Ma'am."

I looked at her hair. *Was it possible she was wearing a wig?*

"I'm behind with the payments."
"Behind with the payments?" I repeated like a parrot.
"Yes Ma'am."
"Do you wear a wig, Virginia?"
"Yes Ma'am."
"Are you wearing a wig now?"
"No Ma'am. It's the wig I bought. I'm behind on my payments. He wants money."

I turned this information over in my mind.

"How much do you owe, Virginia?"
"200 Rand, Ma'am." That represented about four months' wages.
"He's going to get me, Ma'am"
"Get you? You mean, hurt you?"
"Yes Ma'am."
"You're afraid of him?"
"Yes Ma'am."
"Do you have any money at all, Virginia?"
"No Ma'am," she cringed again and then burst into tears.
"If I pay him, will he go away?"
"Yes Ma'am"
"And you owe him 200 Rand?"
"Yes, Ma'am"

    I was stuck between a rock and a hard place. Virginia's wig seemed so trite. My brain told me to send her away with a flea in her ear. I could deduct the money from her monthly wage and maybe she would become more responsible. My heart told me differently. Much of Virginia's miserly monthly wage went back to her Homeland to support her family. If I did not pay the man for the wig, she would be unable to send money home. If I paid the man, he would go away and Virginia's small help to her children would continue.

No help for it, I would have to pay the man for the wig. Anyway, who was I to impose disciplinary measures in these terrible times? Now I knew what was meant by the White Man's Burden.

"If you ask him to come into the kitchen, I will give him R200." I could not see this man accepting a cheque but I had just been to the bank that morning and withdrawn cash for the week's groceries.

Virginia sank down on her knees.

"Thank you, Ma'am. Thank you so much, thank you."

A bit embarrassed, I opened the door and called to the man. He came but I could see he was not comfortable. He doffed his cap and waited.

"My maid, Virginia, tells me she owes you R200 for a wig. Is that so?"
"Yes Ma'am."
"Is that all she owes you?"
"Yes, m."
"Will R200 be full and final payment for the wig?"
"Yes 'm."
"Here is 200 Rand and I do not want to see your face around here again."

The White Man's Burden

*"Do not look where you fell but
where you slipped."*

AFRICAN PROVERB

We were heading for the Pool at the Bryanston Country Club. The front door bell rang. It did not often ring. In fact, it was the first time I had noticed we had a doorbell. Before me on the stoep, stood a tall, well-built middle-aged white man in khaki shorts and shirt with epaulettes, a leather belt ran from his shoulder to his waist, a gun in a holster at his side. He did not look like a boy scout nor did he look like a military man.

"Yes?" I enquired.
"I want to see your bathroom," he replied.

I thought perhaps he had got caught out and wanted to do a pee and then I wondered was it appropriate to let a strange man into the house to do a pee especially one that was wearing a gun. I decided to counter his extraordinary question with one of my own.

"And why would you want to see my bathroom?"
"I want to look at the tiles."

Extraordinarier and extraordinarier – were it not for the gun, I would have closed the door on this crazy lunatic but, under the circumstances, I modified my reaction with a

The White Man's Burden

"Who are you?"
"I'm from the Municipal Tax Department," he answered.

He then handed me his card and I read P. Van der Hog, Sandton Municipal Tax Department.

"I am not the owner of this house," I said. "I rent from the MP for Orange Grove while Parliament is in Cape Town."

"Thank you, Ma'am. I am sure my department is aware of that and will send the tax bill to the owner. I have to see if you have changed the white tiles to colored tiles. If you have, that would be a renovation and would add value to your landlord's property and increase his property taxes."

I allowed Mr. Van der Hog to come in to look at the bathroom. The tiles were white. My landlord would not have to pay more taxes this year. The tax man with the gun departed.

"The best way to eat an elephant in your path is to cut him up into little pieces."
(Meaning: The best way to solve a problem is to take it bit by bit, one at a time.)
AFRICAN PROVERB

On our one acre at Pytchley Road, were empty chicken hutches and chicken runs. It occurred to me that it was an opportunity for the children to experience caring for chickens and eating newly hatched eggs, a total taste experience and something not possible in urban London. After asking neighbors where it would be possible to buy live chickens, they suggested that our garden boy, Philemon, would likely know the answer. He did. With Philemon, we drove into the countryside to a small farm and bought three chickens. Philemon, in the back seat, held three writhing, cackling chickens by their legs.

We put our acquired 'pets' into their new home. Days and months went by; no eggs appeared. Must be out of season, we reasoned, must need a rooster; must be the wrong laying cycle, must be too old, too young. The day after returning from a trip to the Cape, I noticed there were only two chickens in the yard.

"We had three chickens, Philemon. Where is the third?"
"Don't know, Ma'am."

Returning from a weekend at the Kruger National Park, we found one, lonely, chicken.

"Philemon, where is the other chicken?"
"Don't know, Ma'am."

On a weekend when we went to visit the son and family of my Uncle Mac in Ladysmith, Natal, we returned to find – yes, you have guessed it, no chickens.

"Philemon, we have no chickens. Why?"
"Don't know, Ma'am."

The White Man's Burden

About the complete absence of a single new-laid egg?

"Don't know, Ma'am."

"A bird will always use another bird's feathers to feather its own nest."

AFRICAN PROVERB

CHAPTER 6

Diary of a Bored Housewife

September 20th, 1978

Diary, I am a bored housewife. A woman can take only so much pampering. With my house clean and my gardening done, the two older children at school and Rosemary, my maid, in love with the baby, what is there for me to do? I am feeling bored and in need of stimulation.

This particular morning reading the daily Johannesburg Star newspaper, I discovered I was not the only frustrated housewife in South Africa. The writer gives a good idea of how it was for an intelligent woman in 1978 South Africa.

ARE YOU A BORED AND SPOILT HOUSEWIFE?

For the past four years, I have lived with my husband and children in the northern suburbs of Johannesburg. We have a reasonable house and garden and employ a full-time maid and garden boy. My husband is very well paid and we have no financial problems. Then why am I returning to work? This, I hope, will give the answer to my 'friends' who are murmuring, "She must be desperate for money, excitement, status, etc. etc."

Well, girls, I just cannot take this life of endless leisure for another year. I feel like the retired captain of industry who suddenly finds all he has to command is a golf ball. However, I am not 65, I am 35 and I was never even a sergeant of industry!

During my four years stagnation, I think I have tried it all from hysterectomy-ridden tennis clubs to the classy little French cookery classes. You name it and I have had the time and spare cash to do it.

Fancy an Austrian painted chair, a decoupage ostrich egg, a macramé wall hanging, a birthday cake with iced moth orchids, or a quick yoga lotus position and I'm your girl!

How about shopping? I think I have graduated with honors. I have trailed with my friends from Rosebank to Sandton, from Sandton to Hyde Park, from Hyde Park to town all in one morning, to track down that special little pair of winter boots!

So ladies after four years, I decided either I return to work or I roll up my sleeves, dismiss the maid and revert to being a full-time housewife. As my maid is excellent, it seemed stupid to add to the growing number of black unemployed so I found myself a job. Fortunately, I am qualified.

It has not been easy. I was amazed at my first-day nerves, staggered at how tired I felt at the end of the day, flabbergasted at my husband's pride in his new working wife and, most of all, so grateful that my employer could see that I still had 'possibilities'.

Yes, dear friends, I do pay 66% tax but I almost, only almost, pay it gladly. I now feel I have something worth getting out of bed for. I feel part of life and even – salute the flag – a vital cog in the South African economic machine.

My job cannot be done by a man or a black so I do not feel guilty about taking it. My children return home after me so they are not neglected. Even my husband is spared having to indulge in too much after-supper conversation as I no longer have the need to feed vicariously on his daily doings.

I somehow still have the time, energy and interest to pursue certain hobbies which I now thoroughly enjoy, especially as they no longer seem like 'occupational therapy'. Well there, in a macramé-covered ostrich egg, you have it. So dear tight-trousered, manicured, tennis-elbowed and womb-less friends, don't call me, I'll call you.

The Star Newspaper, Johannesburg

I had done the macramé thing and the painted ostrich egg. I had taken thrice-weekly tennis lessons and I was no better a tennis player than when I began. Repeatedly, my tennis coach would chide me, "You're rooted to the ground like a tree, Judith; in tennis you gotta *move*." A lady who had a tennis court in her garden advertised the opening of a 'Bad Tennis Players Club'. Her tennis court was in need of re-surfacing and she hoped to mitigate the cost of its repair. I enthusiastically joined the Bad Tennis Players Club thinking I would not be shamed in the company of players who were as bad as or worse than me. However, I was to find out bad tennis players cannot a tennis game make. Bad tennis players spend so much time apologizing to one another for mis-hits, net cords, out of court serves, locating lost balls over neighbors' fences, there is neither time nor energy to actually play the game. With no good role model to set the pace, there is no incentive to improve. My tennis skills did not improve. The Bad Tennis Players Club came and went. Sadly, I do not think the tennis court owner made enough for a tennis racket never mind the cost of a new asphalt floor.

Since I did not have a work permit, getting a job was not an option. In the 1970s women were coming into their own as teacher, nurse, librarian or as secretary as I had been in London. You worked until you began to show in pregnancy and then you quit. A flight attendant, then called an Air Hostess, who fell in love with her Captain kept the wedding ring well concealed. However, there were some plusses for the yesteryear. One such plus was it did not take two incomes to own a house and a middle-class mom who wanted to stay at home to raise her family did have that option.

In South Africa, it remained two women in the kitchen, sometimes manageable often clashing. As Shakespeare put it in Henry VIII, "two women placed together makes cold weather."

In Johannesburg, white Madams volunteered in the churches, art galleries, museums, the SPCA, whiled away their days on the golf course, tennis court, the bridge four, book club, choir, preserve-making, knitting for black babies, the hairdresser, a manicure, pedicure, high-fashion shopping at the mall and not to forget the inevitable macramé and painted ostrich eggs. It was a hectic social life of weekday coffees, lunches and weekend braais with family and friends around the garden pool. It was all quite delightful and fun but I needed something more, something useful and meaningful. I wondered if there were any fulfilling volunteer opportunities.

At a play date with Elizabeth at the home of my neighbor, the surgeon's wife, the conversation turned to her volunteer work at the Centre for Concern. I discovered this was a church-based organization, which provided practical skills to unemployed maids and garden boys. Madams seeking a maid gave preference to the maid where they could check with the previous employer for a good character reference, a résumé. Unemployed domestic workers with no track-record of experience, no references from a previous Madam, stood little chance of getting a job. The Centre for Concern operated a program for unemployed blacks that provided training in domestic skills, cooking, housekeeping, and gardening and a Certificate of Completion for those who stayed the four months of classes. It sounded like something I might like to do.

At 9.30 each Wednesday morning, twenty unemployed maids and garden boys turned up at the Centre for Concern. They came to learn how to wash, cut, slice, dice vegetables, the correct kitchen knives to use for cutting, carving, slicing. They were taught how to knead flour and butter into short-crust pastry, flaky pastry, puff pastry, Some Madams had their maids bake by hand but some kitchens had kitchen appliances, the timer, mixer, toaster, and the juicer. They were taught appropriate oven temperatures for roasts, casseroles, meringues. Madams would expect formal place-settings (knives graduating in size from the right, forks from the left, dessert spoons pointing to the left), side plates on the left and folded linen napkins sometimes into novelty shapes. Volunteers at the Centre for Concern taught future employees how to wait table, to serve from the diner's left and the domestic arts of sewing, ironing and polishing silver. Participants learned how to shine shoes, fold shirts, wash nappies, make beds with hospital corners, use appropriate cleaning products for fridge and oven, vacuum carpets, clean windows, disinfect and clean toilets, light wood fires, take phone messages for the Madam or Master. Male students learned how to use hand and motor-mowers, hedge-cutters, seed rotators, planting, pruning, hoeing, dead heading, hose-watering, fruit picking, changing an electric bulb, screwdrivers, hammers, tacks, flicking the fuse panel, changing a tire and washing cars. A completed course at the Center for Concern gave the graduate market skills and opportunity to compete on the employment lineup. The 'piece of paper', the Certificate of Graduation confirming these skills, was not a guarantee to a job but it was a help towards it.

White Madams had high expectations of their employees. Black servants should be able to cook traditional Afrikaner dishes such as bobotie, boerewors, sosaties, melktert and pampoemoes in addition to English dishes, lamb roasts, shepherd's pie, toad in the hole, apple and lemon meringue pies. I heard of a madam who fired her maid because she could not cook kedgeree, a fish dish usually eaten at breakfast. To be honest, it was also likely the big draw to this program was the good lunch the maids and garden boys cooked and ate at the Centre and often the left-overs they took home; entirely understandable when one is unemployed and hungry. At the end of the four months, those still with the course were given the ultimate award, the Certificate of Graduation. I got to know the participants individually and to hear sad stories. I heard of madams who were tyrants, hard task masters, yelled at their maid, slapped them, belittled everything they did, accused the maid of stealing earrings, underwear, only to find the item next day. I also heard of good relations with madams, of kindness, concern, help beyond the call of duty, even love. I heard from maids who raised good values in white children and of maids who grieved for madams who had passed away or left the country.

Some students had working husbands and children living close by in a nearby township but mainly the husbands were unemployed. The children of most students were far away in the Homelands looked after by grandma.

A common denominator in the black population was the casual, easy going, *mañana* attitude that came to them so naturally. They laughed, smiled, and clowned and were so profoundly accepting, it was a joy to be with them. I was proud of their motivation to work hard for their goal to complete the program. I also felt fulfilled in my part in helping to make this possible.

Churches had separate white or black congregations, Catholic, Dutch Reform, Anglican, Presbyterian or Evangelist. I cannot recall, or never knew, the denomination of the Centre for Concern but it was definitely a church with an entirely black congregation. At the Graduation Ceremony my next-door neighbor, another volunteer and I were the only white people among roughly one hundred and fifty black congregants. Now, I had an answer to those in London who proffered critical opinions to us for going to a racist country. I knew I could tell them that the work of the Center of Concern enabled black South Africans to come to know that there were well-intentioned and concerned, non-racist white South Africans, that in my own small way I had helped more than if I had not gone. Oh, and diary, I should not leave out that I was no longer a bored housewife!

At the packed Graduation Ceremony at the Centre for Concern, students of the church's program for black employment were in the limelight for the first time in their lives. Wearing blue mortarboards and gowns, they walked proudly to the pulpit to receive their Certificates from the Bishop. I will never forget the singing in the church that day, the voices of South Africa's sons and daughters soaring in sublime harmony while the country rumbled with injustice. It was unlike any singing I have ever heard before or since, a glorious choral combination, utterly moving, heavenly. I will remember the singing of 'African Dream', for the rest of my life.

> Cause in my African Dream
> There's a new tomorrow.
> Cause' in my African Dream
> There's a dream that we can follow.

If it had been Harvard students graduating that day, there would have been no difference in pride of achievement except that I knew these graduates were not moving on to a world where they could reach for the sky, even if the will was there, but into one of servile degradation.

CHAPTER 7

Power Point Presentation
'Ridicularity'

- The operators of a gas station in rural South Africa accepted payment for gas from a black woman but refused the key to the toilet. The toilets were for whites only.

- Motels catered only for whites. For blacks, a long car-drive had to be nonstop.

- Blacks could stay in luxury hotels that they could not afford but not in more modestly priced hotels.

- Blacks could join sports clubs but they could not take part in social activities because the laws prohibited blacks and whites drinking together.

- Blacks were barred from attending the same schools as whites but the Government turned a blind eye to blacks attending private schools.

- In a system of color classification, black people were 'Africans'; mixed races including Chinese were classified 'colored'; 'Indians were 'Asians'; Japanese were classified as white; Whites were called 'Europeans.'

- A test to find out your race was to run a pencil through your hair. If the pencil stayed in place, this indicated you must be of kinky-haired black stock. If the pencil slid through your hair, you could be considered white. Blacks who wanted to be reclassified as 'colored' could undergo the pencil test: if the pencil fell out when you shook your head, you could become 'colored'.

- If the moons of your fingernails were a bit more mauve than white, this indicated a hint of black blood.

- Black people had passbooks, white people had passports.

- Being white meant your kids got free schooling; being black meant you paid for your kids schooling.

- Being black meant your kids could become teachers, nurses, doctors, lawyers but they could only offer their services to other blacks.

CHAPTER 8

Victoria Avenue, Kensington B.

During our four-month assignment in South Africa, we lived in Pytchley Road, Bryanston. Somehow, along the way things changed. Although Philip was completing his assignment on time, he was given more tasks from head office and the allotted four months became two years. Anyway, in truth, neither of us were ready to return. Who would want to leave this paradise, this life of luxury, the kids bronzed and happy? We could enjoy a few more braais. More than that, we wanted to see more of South Africa particularly the Western Cape. Unabashedly, I admit we dragged out our time for as long as we could.

For the remainder of our assignment, we rented a house on Victoria Avenue, Kensington 'B' in a suburb of Randburg, north of Johannesburg. To drive through Kensington 'B' was to blink an eye, the usual conventional shops, the butcher, the grocer, the gas station, pleasant treed avenues; houses set behind high brick walls much like Pytchley Road except now the lots were not five acres but half an acre. Logic should have it that somewhere was a Kensington 'A.' Hard as we tried, we could not find Kensington 'A' and neither could we find just simple 'Kensington'. Years later using the technology of 'Google Earth', I located a suburb called Kensington about thirty-three kilometers from 'Kensington 'B.' How could we have missed it? Maybe Kensington 'A' was a Brigadoon, the Scottish town that re-appears once every hundred years. Google Earth described a Kensington with no letter tag as an upbeat, trendy locale with a collection of artisans.

This second house was also a ranch bungalow and, by luck, it was in the Bryandale Primary School catchment area, the school that had been stamped into our British passports. The kids did not have to change school for which I was eternally grateful. I cannot imagine the officialdom and fuss we would have had to endure had it been necessary to change school – likely our passports would have been revoked and the family deported!

This time we found a house to satisfy all our needs, four bedrooms and a swimming pool. The living room was imaginatively furnished with the clean lines of contemporary design, a modern three-seat sectional and love seat. Beneath the glass coffee table was a Zebra-hide rug complete with legs and tail. On the far wall, centre stage, was a brick fireplace, either side of which were shelves not filled with books this time, but with exquisite African *objets d'art*, statuesque and graceful, pleasing to the eye. To describe these artworks is beyond difficult but in my mind's eye I have two cleverly intertwined giraffes, a truly noble ebony bull elephant, a ceramic angel riding the back of a whale, two dancers locked in love, a tall, twisting hand-painted ceramic vase and at either end of the mantelpiece a hand-carved ebony candlestick. Hanging on one wall was a woven tapestry depicting Zulu warriors dancing. The inevitable macramé project made to hold a goldfish bowl or was it a pot of flowers, contained neither and hung limply from a hook in the ceiling. In one corner was a large black leather beanbag that Nicholas subsequently adopted as his personal seat. He was always to be found on his beanbag. When out of the beanbag the contours of his shape could be seen in it; it was his special place. I have a photo of him in the beanbag absorbed in a book, The Making of a Surgeon. At eleven, Nicholas was on track to do the things we always knew he would. He did not become a surgeon but his interest in medicine continued via neuro-psychology at a major Canadian Hospital.

On window shelves around the house stood cool *avant-garde* ornaments, sculpted figurines in soapstone, marble or wrought iron. We worried that these valuable items would be tempting to the little fingers of Elizabeth, approaching two. Elizabeth was late in walking and shuffled around on her bottom – the valuable artifacts would be safe for now.

In the bathroom was a photo of Yoko Ono and John Lennon, nude, with fig leaves, real fig leaves, covering their nether parts. Lift the fig leaf, reveal the glory.

I had given little thought to the abstract painting hanging in the main hall other than it was attractive and colorful until Philip said to me, "Take a closer look, look hard." I looked hard and the painting revealed itself to me as an ingenious complex design of intertwined couples in varying intimate sexual poses. The picture put me in mind of the 3D abstract images that were trendy a few years ago, an image within an image, visible only if you focused your eyes so hard, they glazed over. Needless to say, I did not mention this discovery to the children!

We never met the owners of this house but the eccentricities and appurtenances of the furniture and pieces profiled two younger adults, bohemian types, from academia, intellectual and artsy. In fact, our landlords were two Professors at Witwatersrand University on sabbatical leave in the United States. I could not find one conventional adjective to describe any item in the house. Come with me on a tour. We will start with the garden.

At the front entrance, a little arched wood door was just visible between two high brick walls. As I opened the door, this time no garden boy met me as at Pytchley Road. However, something else was there to meet me. Lurking behind that garden door was an indigenous plant predator, a giant cactus with sharp spikes eagerly waiting to snare a wayward passerby. It took a few good scratches until we learned to avoid the big fellow. The garden was alive with native shrubs, plants, trees, yuccas, cacti, paved walkways, so much so there was zero room for weeds; a well-planned garden requiring very little care and no need of a garden boy.

A few days later while checking for letters in the mailbox, behind the garden entrance door, we discovered a surprise package. A lizard had made its home in our mailbox. Each time we retrieved mail, we had to disturb the little lizard and return it to its home before closing the mailbox. Nicholas would put the lizard on his shoulder while he took out the mail.

To the right of the house was a latched gate leading to a fenced swimming pool. In our lease was a clause relating to a plant at the edge of the pool requiring special care. The lease referred to a plant of prehistoric nature and we were asked to take particular care to ensure its survival. This was the theory. In practice I could see nothing about the plant that needed care. It did not grow, it did not bud. It did not need watering. The valuable plant took good care of itself. The result was simply to cause me to worry and make frequent journeys to check on the plant's condition. If anything had happened to that plant by dint of accident or nature, I fear we would have been on the hook but quite how to compensate for a dead or damaged prehistoric plant, I have no idea and I was glad not to find out!

Prolific plant life and greenery interlaced the sculpted rocks and boulders sloping down to the pool edge. It was a small secluded swimming pool in a pretty setting. A waterfall cascaded down the rocks setting up a rippling effect in the pool below. Small yellow and green Weaverbirds visited the area frequently and built nests in the trees around the pool. Weaverbird nests hang upside down, the Weaverbird entering its nest from underneath to feed its chicks. The upside-down nests built into branches overhanging the pool were the cause of many tragedies as chicks fell out of nests into the pool. Stupid birds!

Huge African Bullfrogs resided round the pool. Bullfrogs can weigh three pounds or more and can bite if disturbed. None of us were actually bitten but we were careful to stay well clear of them. We also had a couple of Giant Toads. I was quite taken with Giant Toads, such ugly devils, what was the great man in the sky thinking when he designed them? Occasionally snakes, garter snakes, harmless, would slither between the rocks to slide away as fast as they came. The frogs at the pool attracted the snakes; the snakes ate the frogs – predator and prey – the chain of life. I knew neighbors with frog-infested pools. One neighbor put a toy clockwork plastic snake into his pool which wiggled around and, incredibly, the frogs fled.

To the left of the house was another area of garden. Here was the play area used by our landlord's children; a children's slide and a sandpit bordered by a low circular brick wall. Within the wall was an assortment of plastic spades, sieves and buckets. There was the shell of an old red Messerschmitt Bubble car from the 1960s, its engine removed. Bubble cars of the era had three wheels and one entry door which opened upwards with the steering wheel and dashboard attached. All that was left of the car were its seats, dashboard and steering wheel. On a cub scout outing, Nicholas had ridden his two-wheel bicycle on the famed Kyalami Grand Prix race track which was then, and is still today, a premier motor racing circuit. The little bubble car in our garden became a vehicle for invention and imagination to a boy dreaming of roaring up a Formula 1 Ferrari. There was a wooden playhouse with stable-type half-doors equipped with cup boards, shelves, a play stove, a wooden bed, pots and pans, a tea set, dolls and small toys. It was an Alice in Wonderland, a Peter Pan garden. We had so lucked out.

I noticed there were no windows at the front of the house. Over the years of our marriage, I have been the recipient of spontaneous scientific discourses from Philip, an ex-student of London's Imperial College of Science. I learnt that the absence of windows at the front of the house was because the house faced south and that this was a deliberated architectural plan to keep the house cool in summer and insulated in winter. Most houses in the Transvaal, I was told, had no windows at the front. Please do not query this.

At the centre of the house was an Atrium open to the sky filled with evergreen native plants, yuccas, varieties of ferns, silvery shrubs, flowers of white and yellow, large prickly bushes. Wisteria climbed a trellis fence, a whiff of mint, chamomile and lavender. There were real banana trees growing in the atrium. I always thought bananas turned bright yellow when they ripened. The bananas in our atrium became a brownish yellow. It is possible our bananas were plantains not bananas? When I lamented to a visitor that our bananas were not doing well, she explained that, indeed, they were doing very well. She said that bananas in fruit stores turn an artificial yellow. As with houses having no windows in the front, I would take this news about store bananas with a pinch of salt! The atrium was self-contained and entered by a glass door from the hallway. African folk law has it that mosquitoes are not attracted to the skin of babies up to a year. Whether this is true or not I do not know but I never knew Elizabeth to get a mosquito bite. The summer hot humid conditions within the Atrium made for a lovely home for mosquitoes. I tended to avoid the Atrium in the summer months; mosquitoes are attracted to me. It would have been nice to have seen humming birds there, nature's flying machines, so interesting to watch.

Blooms of sweetly smelling pink bougainvillea straddled the roof as we made our way down the garden path to greet Rosemary, our new maid. This time, the house had not come with a maid. We had to find our own live-in help. By coincidence, an employee at Philip's company was returning to the UK and his maid needed a job. Rosemary had been working for this couple for eight years and they gave a glowing reference particularly as nanny to their four children. Had I been volunteering at the Centre for Concern, I can think of many delightfully warm women to fill the position to which I would have had no hesitation offering the job.

Television did not come to South Africa until 1976. The National Government had feared it would corrupt the nation. We arrived just two years later and South African television was still in its infancy, half a day in English and half a day in Afrikaans. We decided to brave it out, go without television. The South African Broadcasting Company turned down a TV commercial for the Walt Disney cartoon movie: "The Rescuers" because they felt the expression "holy mackerel" was irreverent!

LOOK WHAT THEY'VE BANNED NOW

THE SABC has turned down a TV commercial for a Walt Disney cartoon because it contains the expression "holy mackerel". The commercial's advertising agents were told this week that the trailer, for Disney's "The Rescuers" was unacceptable because of these words. "Where possible, the phrase, 'holy-Mackerel' should be avoided in commercials: said the SABC, "as its repetition could create a negative reaction." The offending words are used by one of the film's characters – a mouse.

This is the second time in a week that the SABC has rejected a commercial. The first was a radio spot in which novelist Harold Robbins promoting the film of his novel, "The Betsy", said: I write about money, sex and power.

The White Man's Burden

> We weren't altogether amazed at that decision, said the film company's publicity director, since we know that sex is a sore point at Auckland Park. But we really did think that fish were Innocuous, whatever their level of divinity.

The radio provided quality programming. Particularly good were the radio plays. A radio play involves the listener's imagination far more than a stage play or a movie, as does a book. I first heard 'The Monkey's Paw' on South African radio, a classic story of supernatural suspense about a couple possessing a dried-up relic of a monkey's paw. The story goes that anyone who owns the monkey's paw is granted three wishes but the wishes come at great personal sacrifice. In the story, the couple's first wish was for wealth. The wish was fulfilled from the proceeds of a life insurance policy following the death of their son in a mining accident. The second wish was for the son to come back to life. In the radio play, the imagination goes into overdrive visualizing the broken, bloodied body of the accident-disfigured, zombie son, lurching up the garden path to the closed front door. At the very moment the son knocks at the front door, the terrified parents make their third and final wish which is granted – to have the son returned to the peace of his grave.

Johannesburg is 6,000 feet above sea level. As such, it never gets too hot or too cold. It is a perfect climate and, as one would expect in a perfect climate, South Africans lead a very outdoor life. The only problem I had with the perfect climate was that, hard as I tried, I could not get meringue to rise and crisp up. The saying was it had something to do with the difference in air pressure because of Johannesburg's height above sea level. I have not been able to find scientific evidence of this and assume it is more likely a product of my poor cooking!

We would regularly eat outdoors around our 'braai', BBQ, or at friends' braais, cooking up steaks and sosaties, curried meat grilled on skewers. We joined the Sunday social set of long rounds of entertaining at our home or at friends' braais and swimming pools. It was all new to us; delightful in the short-term but I rather thought I might get bored of endless braais.

Philip and I were long-time amateur thespians, me a stagehand and he an actor anything from Cassius in Julius Caesar to Neil Simon comedies. So far as we knew, there was no outlet for amateur theatre hobbyists in Kensington B or Randburg. It could have been, of course, that as newbies we had not come across it. However, it is usual for amateur theatre to find its way into the remotest corners.

South Africa's school 'marbles season' was marble mania. Marbles ranged in size from midget to huge. There were plain glass, single color marbles and marbles with deep, complex inter-woven colors. A marble's worth was its size and eye-appeal and, indeed, one could be spellbound peering into the depths of a little glass multi-colored ball. You had to know your jargon to play this game. At the time, I was not into marbles so I knew little about the game except I heard words like 'Junkies.', 'Ironies,', 'Goons.' or 'Goonies'. I learned the game was on when the kids 'knuckled down' to 'toss the shooter'. Kids had their own very personal collections. If you were a good player, you had a bigger collection, larger marbles and marbles that were more interesting to look at. Playing marbles was intense and competitive, played as a school break-time activity like skipping or hopscotch. I bought Nicholas a starter kit, which he guarded zealously.

It was good to see Nicholas and his school friend Ralph hanging around together, and also to know that Karen was friends with Ralph's younger sister, Cavil. Ralph lived about twenty minutes from our place and rode his bike to our house. Nicholas had been a biker in London and we needed to get him a bike. The roads to Ralph's house were long and wide, the houses on estates of five-acres, a five-minute walk between each house. Nicholas was used to the narrow roads of London Ealing with cars lining each side of the road, drivers having to stop to negotiate who goes first. In Kensington B, the bus service was sparse. In fact, I do not remember ever riding a bus in the two years we lived in South Africa or, indeed, if the kids ever did. Moms were stay-at-home moms, their life's mission to chauffeur the kids to and from school and to their friends. I was already doing enough driving to school and back, to playmates and to cubs and brownies. However, the local topography was very different to that of flat Ealing. Ralph's house was at the top of a hill, a very steep climb. Given a week or two, Nicholas's leg muscles would have propelled him up the hill easily but at the start, that hill was hard work.

Across from Ralph's house lived two older Afrikaner teenagers who watched the new boy struggling up the hill. Bullies are quick to latch on to limitations and Ralph's new English friend was the perfect target. Perhaps it was because the boy was new to South Africa, perhaps it was because the boy was English not Afrikaner, perhaps it was because he could not climb the hill, perhaps it was because they were bigger, taller, stronger, older.

The White Man's Burden

Whatever the reason, these two teens saw Nicholas as an ideal pick-on. The Afrikaners taunted Nicholas, took his bike riding it near and far; threatened to sell it or ride it to the nearby garbage tip. Sometimes they took the bike away for long periods and left Nicholas not knowing how to get home, stranded. Around six o'clock in the Transvaal, the sun starts its journey towards dusk, and Nicholas worried he would not make it home before dark. When he rode to Ralph's house, it was as if the Afrikaners were expecting him, waiting for him, threatening him every time. What makes a bully, who knows? Some say the bully is a victim too, a victim of a dysfunctional family, of being unloved, uncared for, or in South Africa at the time, the victim of an environment of aggressive Apartheid racism.

Whatever was the cause, first and foremost bullies are cowards.

The numerous episodes of harassment took its toll on Nicholas. Our time in South Africa was drawing to a close. Instead of feeling sad at leaving his good friend, he was beginning to feel relieved. After one particularly nasty bout of bullying, Ralph decided it was time to set things right for his friend and for the Afrikaner teens to get their come-uppance, to up the ante as it were. And so it was full-on war, two Afrikaner teens against two boys, one British English, one South African and a secret weapon – Ralph had a pellet gun!

Those who have seen the movie A Christmas Story will be familiar with the classic taunt, "You'll shoot your eye out!" By coincidence, the leading character in the movie is also named Ralph; a boy who wants a BB air gun for Christmas. BB guns are bought

The White Man's Burden

as toys for children and are not thought to inflict injury. A good pair of jeans can withstand the impact of a pellet shot. It was quite usual in South Africa for boys to have pellet guns. Ralph's plan was to take the Afrikaner teens by surprise. Ralph and Nicholas fired pellet after pellet at the teens. There was no doubt of their intent, but the pellets missed their targets. As cowards do, the teens fled to safety behind a corrugated iron metal wall. Ralph's pellet shots continued to rain down on them ricocheting off the metal wall. The teens were stuck behind the wall, rendered inactive and they made a break for the refuge of their house. An enraged African bull is not to be taken lightly and neither was the Afrikaner father who stormed over to Ralph's house to berate Ralph's mother about her son's behavior. Ralph's mother stood her ground firmly. Wisely, she had told the boys to hide in the back seat of the Mercedes in the garage as she attempted to reason and calm the father. The boys had no idea what took place between Ralph's mother and the bullies' dad. Whatever it was, there was no further trouble from the Afrikaner teens. Nicholas continued to be wary when he rode to Ralph's house but he enjoyed the climb, the feel of the power of his muscles and felt sorry to be leaving his good friend Ralph. To this day, Nicholas still loves to ride the open roads of the Vancouver, Canada, coastline.

Philip had a business colleague, with a teenage son, who invited Nicholas to shoot pigeons with more sophisticated air guns than pellet guns. In Johannesburg, flocks of pigeons pervade the skies and killing pigeons is the everyman's hobby. Rock pigeons roost in the city on tall buildings and then swoop down to seek seeds in the parks. Nicholas remembers actually landing a pigeon. I detest killing for sport but am willing to compromise if it is for hygiene or consumption. The urban pigeon is a pest and its droppings a health risk. I reluctantly conceded to him pigeon shooting. The friend asked Nicholas to stay for supper after the pigeon shooting. On the menu, pigeon pie! Wing shooting is the name given to the sport of killing wild birds in South Africa. In 2017, gun licensing of all firearms in South Africa is conditional on a competency test, background check and inspection of owner's premises.

Friends, clients and business colleagues invited us to many braais and we were overdue in reciprocating hospitality. We extended invites for a lunch time Pizza Party with appetizers, pizza, salads and desserts. This was before the days of pizza store take-outs and home deliveries. I made the pizzas the day before. A couple of hours before the guests were due to arrive, I took the pizzas out of the fridge, cut them into slices and put them in the pantry. When I went to retrieve them for reheating in the oven, to my horror I discovered they were crawling with ants. It was Sunday and Sunday was Lord's Day, the stores closed. Panic! What was I to do? At this point I had a moral dilemma. What was best practice for a hostess in a critical situation like this? Do I go out there and yell "the pizza has ants on it but lots of Vitamin C?" In some cultures, insects are a nutritious and a delicious delicacy. Unfortunately, South Africa is not one of them. I had to make a decision. A helpful old cliché came to mind – "What the eye doesn't see, the heart doesn't grieve over." I spent the next half hour carefully picking ants off the pizzas before putting them into the oven. Feigning normality, I watched, nervously, the faces of guests for signs of disgust – and ants! It was then I had an epiphany. I salved my conscience with a sobering thought. Reheating in the oven would have any remaining ants well cooked and any bad stuff knocked out of them. Cooked insects would be safe but I should own up, I ate no pizza myself!

The White Man's Burden

We spent more than a year in Victoria Avenue through a South African winter. From early evening to early morning, the temperature would fluctuate. In the middle of the night, it could drop to zero. Early morning, we wore sweaters over T-shirts and, as the day warmed up, removed a layer and then another until by noon we were down to tee shirts and shorts. The reverse procedure started around 4 pm, putting back layers, sweaters and long pants, as the temperature fell.

Elizabeth would go missing from time to time to be found in Rosemary's room, just off the kitchen. The maid's room is customarily a no-no for the Madam. However, on a mission to retrieve Elizabeth, I glimpsed a chest of drawers and a single bed. What really caught my eye was the pile of bricks under each leg of the bed raising the bed about six-inches off the floor. I wondered why but it left my mind. Sometime later,  I was with a South African white Madam who was ranting on about her bad luck with maids and how the Tokoloshe must have come. Not understanding what she said, I asked her to repeat the word. "The Tokoloshe" she said, "you know that evil spirit that comes to get them." Subsequently, I was to hear more about the Tokoloshe, a black superstition about an evil spirit called upon by malevolent people to cause trouble for others. Apparently, it is very fond of women and resembles a tiny, hairy dwarf. In raising her bed, Rosemary was protecting herself from the, Tokoloshe, who was too small to climb up her bed. To my astonishment, I found the superstition prevailed among white Afrikaner women too.

On winter evenings the temperature dipped. It could go to zero. Snow is a rare occurrence in South Africa. In the twentieth century, Wikipedia lists 22 days of snow in the last 103 years. Rosemary had never seen snow and I found her curiously studying a Christmas card from England. There was one small boiler in the dining room to heat the whole house. We were low in fuel for the boiler. Philomen knew where we could replenish supplies. Philip and I drove to Alexandra, a nearby township. It was a shanty town of corrugated iron shacks, a sad, depressing sight of poverty and depravity– men, women and children, idle, hungry and unmotivated through unemployment. The streets were narrow, some only a meter wide with a few stores, shebeens, communal water points and banks of chemical toilets. The riots of 1976 that started in Soweto also spread to Alexandra where nineteen people were killed. In early Apartheid, 'black spots' near to white suburbs were bulldozed to the ground to force the black population to the newly established eleven Homelands. Alexandra Township escaped, saved because of the friendship between an Alexandra church minister and a National Government Cabinet Minister.

The newspaper was full of stories of home invasions. Our house at Victoria Street had no gate security or guard dog. During our stay on Victoria Street, maybe we were lucky, but we did not experience any criminal activity nor did we hear of other local home invasions. It was very different in other African states such as Nigeria, Zambia and Kenya where crime was running amok. Apartheid was, without doubt, a heinous atrocity; if it had any benefit, it was the presence of solid policing and the crackdown on crime. The Bantu and white police were strong and diligent in maintaining law and order. We did not live with a gun under our pillow, and as far as we knew, nor did our neighbors.

Many years later in Canada, at dinner at a neighbor's house, I was talking about South Africa and the house on Victoria Street, the zebra rug and the shameful painting. To my astonishment, the two other couples sitting at the dining table were able to depict exactly the *objects d'art* I was describing. How could that be? As the conversation progressed, it turned out all three couples sitting at that table had rented the same house in Victoria Street, Kensington B, Randburg South Africa, but in different years. It was an extraordinary coincidence, a most weird, fluky experience. There was much hilarity and conversation about the hot, sexy picture and the bathroom fig leaves.

CHAPTER 9

Different and Differences

The best known story in the world is that of Adam and Eve and their enforced departure from the Garden of Eden. If it were not for the first lady eating the forbidden apple, we might all be whiling away our days in paradise shamelessly naked in the sun, no wicked freezes, no earthquakes, tsunamis, wars, disease, no money and consequently no greed. I reckon here in South Africa, I am as close as I will ever be to a Garden of Eden. The Israelites wandered forty years in the wilderness. Forty is a significant number biblically, biologically, historically, politically and personally. Forty days is the time allotted to Lent; Noah's flood lasted forty days; the fetus takes forty days to be discernable in the womb; 'the forty year itch'; forty winks; I was forty when I went to Johannesburg and it took forty-six years for Nelson Mandela to bring democracy to South Africa.

The incessant dreary grey skies of London are fading memories giving way to cloudless blue, my new norm. Through the window of my South African kitchen, I see palm and bamboo trees, succulents, cacti, bananas and lemon trees, a swimming pool and a plant of pre-historic value.

I usually absorb consistent background noise as part of the daily pattern of life until the birds stop singing when I am instantly alert to the silence. The daily regular quiet at 4 pm portends a darkening sky, flashes of lightning, bolts of thunder that shake the very marrow of your bones, precipitating a torrential rainfall with large puddles left where none had been before. Half an hour later, a few residual raindrops fall from the leaves. All is as it was, not a sign that nature so violently paid a visit, not a puddle remains, the sky once more blue and cloudless, the air lingering with the warm earthy smells so uniquely African. Hosts and guests 'braaing' on a Sunday afternoon, who had sought refuge in the house, now return to the braai. All is normal, just summer in the Transvaal.

During the daily thunderstorm, our brave protector and defender Alex the guard-dog shivers and shakes pathetically. I take pity on him and allow him into the house where he seeks comfort under the bedclothes in the master bedroom. Allowing Alex, the outdoor guard dog into the house, notwithstanding the master bedroom, is very naughty and, doubtless, a breach of our lease.

During my two years in the warm climes of South Africa, I found black South Africans to be easy going, laid-back, affable – maybe the warmer the weather, the warmer the people. Think back to Canadian winters or more to the winters of Nunavut where it snows from September to May. I wondered how much sun, warmth and beauty of his native land, an unemployed black African living in squalor would willingly exchange for a job in the blinding blizzards of Iqaluit. When it is cold, it is no problem to don a heavy sweater, to turn up the furnace, and snuggling together is nice. The even temperate climate of Johannesburg, never too hot, rarely too cold, was the perfect climate. Much of South Africa is humid and clammy, move a finger and the sweat pours off. Blame Eve that we cannot run round naked!

In 1979, tiny cracks in the political mirror were beginning to show; minor relaxations of rules but portents of an undercurrent for change. During our short stay, echoes of former British Prime Minister, Harold MacMillan's 'winds of change' blew in a mixed race public swimming pool in Johannesburg, one at Camps Beach, Cape Town and at Port Elizabeth in the Orange Free State.

Theatres and cinemas started applying for mixed-race licenses. Many were turned down. There were watery signs that the National Government had at least awareness that Apartheid was not for the long term; that South Africa was the only developed nation in the world operating a systemic racial policy; that it had to let go some time but it would hang on for now.

"DELAYS ON OPEN THEATRES HITTING SA"

The Government's delay in deciding on applications to open at least 20 South African theatres to all races is damaging this country's image overseas.

The general manager of Johannesburg Civic Theatre said at least 20 applications for open theatres had been sent to the Minister of Community Development, before the April 15th deadline. The call for applications on March 10th was front page news overseas.

The Star newspaper, Johannesburg

In Britain, it was still the High Street lined with butcher, fishmonger, grocer, fruit and vegetable shops, post office, library and local café while in South Africa the concept of the retail mall was emerging. It was a novelty for me to park my car underground and to be able to walk to Sandton Mall to shop the one hundred stores there, all indoors. I no longer walked three miles a day to take the kids to school. We possessed a second company car and I drove the kids to school and home and I cannot deny that having someone to do my housework was utterly sublime.

The drive to pick up the kids from school was a left turn on to Bryanston Road, then a right onto the wide-open main arterial William Nicol Highway. Not a shop, a condominium a tower, an office block, a factory, a petrol garage, blocked the panoramic view over fields, hills and veldt, the rise and fall of the arterial road and its convergence to vanishing point on the horizon. It was rumored the highways in South Africa (or at least those near Johannesburg) had been strengthened to act as airplane runways in case of need for military action.

I had to ensure I arrived early because there was a competition to find a shady parking space beneath the lone tree that stood outside the school. Parked cars radiated from the tree like the spokes of a wheel. If I were late, the spaces would be filled. I, in my car, would bake like a cake in an oven. Nobody walked to school even if they lived fifty yards away, a black African man would likely appear, pointing his finger, "Go home, Ma'am"!

On streets and paths, the earth was orange-red. At first, it intrigued me. Within a few months, the lack of green, dearth of trees, the wide expanses of blandness stretching as far as the eye could see, got to me. I began to yearn for the thick-trunked oak trees of England, its pastures of grazing cows, narrow country lanes and ironically, even the urban striped zebra crossings of Ealing.

Behind the walls of our home, it was a very different scene. Here was a fantasy of color, rich reds, blues, pinks and orange, strelitzia, bougainvillea, the striped red gazania, the candy cane sorrel and the ruby-red and blue 'wine cup' named for its goblet shaped flowers. There was a profusion of trees with fitting names – the pompom tree named for clusters of soft pink pompoms at the tips of its branches, the leopard tree, a slender, delicate tree its trunk dark brown patches against a light background, hence its name and the candelabra tree with branches extending from a central trunk in a three-prong effect like a candelabra.

In London when school was over for the day, the smiley, friendly 'lollypop lady' was a familiar sight carrying aloft her red stop-sign to chaperone her charges across the road. Outside Bryandale Primary School, it was not a lollypop lady but a 'school crossing patrol' comprised of five older students with bright red sashes to designate their official status. Two students were positioned at the nearside curb marshaling the pupils into an orderly queue ready to cross while, at the far curb, two students waited to receive them. The fifth student, the crossing patrol leader, took a stop-pole to the center of the road to halt the oncoming traffic to allow the kids safely to cross the road. Once over the road, the students ran to their parents' parked cars if lucky under the lone tree, if not, to bake in the sun. I was impressed by this student crossing patrol initiative. I thought it gave the kids a sense of responsibility. It would not be stood for in Britain for the very reason it would rob a British homemaker of two-hours a day pay during school time. There is a strong propensity in Britain to protest labor inequity and I could well imagine a National Lollypop Ladies Strike!

I had occasion to use the South African medical service. I was feeling ill. I had no energy, felt like a limp rag. I made an appointment to see a family doctor. The doctor took one look at me, "Hepatitis," he said and added "When you see yourself turning orange, come back to see me." Hepatitis 'A' was very common in South Africa. Today, there is a vaccine. I spent several weeks languishing at home, with sleepless nights, fever, fatigue, loss of appetite, nausea and vomiting but I never turned orange.

When we moved from Bryanston to Kensington B, I showed visitors round our new home. Elizabeth, a plump eighteen months, was still not walking. I carried her on my hip while showing the house to friends, which took its toll on my back. It became serious enough that I was admitted for two weeks bed rest to the Sandton Clinic. After two weeks of bed rest on Demerol, I left hospital pain free. In Canada, exercise is now the prescription for back pain and I believe, if regular targeted exercise had been the prescription then, I would have been saved future recurrences.

In the hospital ward of six beds, I was the only patient on bed-rest, the other five being surgery cases and all were Afrikaners. Finding I did not speak Afrikaans, they agreed to speak English which I found profoundly thoughtful. The Sandton Clinic was a private clinic, the pinnacle of luxury with a first class cuisine, wine served at evening meals. Whether it was cultural, religious or sheer coincidence, the five Afrikaner patients did not imbibe. Despite instructions, the catering staff continued to include a glass of wine with the dinner tray. Another example of African lesson #101, 'Embedded rituals never change,' On Demerol for muscle relaxation and drinking several glasses of wine each evening, I was in some other world! Bed-rest means exactly what it says, not to get out of bed. Bored and ambulatory, I found myself doing small acts of kindness, picking up magazines and papers for those surgical patients confined to bed. I was helping a patient to a glass of water when the very resonant voice of my exceedingly handsome orthopedic surgeon, boomed out, "Mrs. Bogod, get back to bed immediately." I sidled back to bed like a guilty schoolgirl my heart all aflutter!

In 1979, South African hospital nurses wore uniforms that looked nicely professional, khaki tops and pants, a smack of militarism with shoulder epaulettes, the pips and stripes identifying a Charge Nurse, Unit Nurse or a Nurse's Aide. The South African nurses' uniform of 1979 reflected the traditional values, precepts and ideations of the National Government for efficiency and authority. Today nurses in South Africa wear flowery patterned tops just as nurses do in Canada. There is something to be said for a traditional uniform – at least it is not difficult to distinguish a nurse from a patient.

The White Man's Burden

Golda Meir autographs Leonard Schacht's text of "Golda" while my cousin, Thelma Ruby, looks on. Photograph taken in Mrs. Meir's home in Tel-Aviv.

A cousin whom I had never met was a professional actress. Thelma Ruby from Manchester, England, was in Johannesburg playing the title role of Golda Meir, the former Prime Minister of Israel in the play 'Golda' at the Alexandra Theatre in Johannesburg. Thelma came to visit me at the Sandton Clinic. In my drugged state, I have no memory of the visit so, effectively, I have still to meet her. The play opened in Pretoria, South Africa's Capital. The theatre had requested a permit for an all-race audience and been refused. The Israeli Ambassador declined to attend the whites-only performance as, subsequently, did the Ambassadors of the United States, France, Germany, Switzerland, Australia and Sweden. The dissimilarity of laws from cities no more than thirty miles apart gives some idea of the confusion, flux and madness in the political arena.

The White Man's Burden

*"Is there an Ambassador in the House?" A satire of the old Yiddish joke
"Is there a doctor in the house?"*
*(A cartoonist's depiction of the Ambassadorial stand against
Pretoria's whites only theatre.)*

Their Excellences did, however, see the play in a multi-racial theatre in Johannesburg.

Pretoria was a city largely government civil service also predominantly Afrikaans speaking and Afrikaner culture. Almost all of the restaurants in Pretoria city served whites only. In public parks, there were clearly marked benches for whites or non-whites.

113

For Pretoria, the segregation policy was an expensive exercise as it required building separate hospitals, libraries, post offices, hotels and public toilets. Segregation was so extreme white borrowers had their domestic workers return books parceled in wrapping paper to ensure they were clean. Oddly, the system did not apply to banks where the various racial groups could queue together without any problem.

There was a total absence of any social network for whites or black South Africans. However hard as the going got in Britain, I knew the social network would not see me starve. The Johannesburg Press got hold of the story of a British fellow called Mr. Warren dubbed in a British newspaper, the 'Luxton Breeder,' a British dad, father of sixteen children by a former and current wife. There is discussion both for and against Mr. Warren's situation but whatever side you are on here is what a 1978 South Africa newspaper made of it.

'IF HE LIVED HERE, HE'D EITHER WORK OF STARVE'

If Big Daddy, John Warren, lived in South Africa, he'd either work or see his children starve," says a Department of Social Welfare and Pensions Official. And he laughed incredulously at John's antics in the British welfare state. "South Africa is not a welfare state," said the official. "If Mr. Warren lived here, he wouldn't get a cent from us unless he worked. And we don't accept any feeble excuses either." Keeping fit and looking after two wives and 20 children just do not qualify a man for money in the sunny south. He would have to prove to the satisfaction of a district surgeon that he was unable to work. And there would be no question of his staying at home because he couldn't find a job he liked. We will help a man whose salary does not cover the needs of his family, but a man who stays at home gets nothing.

Meanwhile, the British Minister of Social Security told Parliament that, under British Law, a man may claim social security cash for his wife AND mistress. It would be inappropriate to exclude from such arrangements a mistress because she could then claim benefits in her own right at greater cost to public funds. It's a dilly dole world over there.

The Star newspaper, Johannesburg

Animals native to South Africa are often in the news. In Britain, we may be bothered by deer or grey squirrels or, rarely, the venomous adder. In Canada, we invade the territory of deer, bears and cougars that sometimes come back to haunt us. In South Africa, crocodiles and snakes make grand entrances.

CROC AT HIS WINDOW

A man killed a 4 meter crocodile on a farming estate near Johannesburg after it had snapped its jaws at him through his bathroom window. Mr. Viljoen said "crocodiles are seen regularly in the area but this is the first time one has stopped on our lawn."

Afraid that the crocodile would attack his dogs and cats, Mr. Viljoen tried to catch it. But the reptile which lay about 1½ meters from the bathroom window – almost level with the ground – refused to move.

"I dislike killing any animal but with staff arriving in the early morning and in the interest of our eight-year old daughter, it would have been unwise to leave it roaming round the garden." As he opened the window to shout at it, the crocodile lurched forward and snapped its jaws less than a meter from him.

The Star newspaper, Johannesburg

IT'S THE SSSNAKE SSSEASON

It is the height of the snake season and experts today warned people to be more alert to encounters. The Transvaal Snake Park is receiving about 20 reports a day of reptiles in lounges, bedrooms, bathrooms and swimming pools. "Stand still or back away if you can" is the advice of the experts. "A snake is not going to attack you unless you hassle him."

Reptiles are seen more in December and January because they are flushed out by rain and they are also out in search of prey.

Comfortable as sandals may be, it would be a better idea to wear something more protective if you are walking through bush area.

The Star newspaper, Johannesburg

Moving from bangers and mash, toad-in-the-hole, boiled cabbage to sosaties and boerewors, South Africa's diverse food palate is a giant leap of the taste buds – sourced from the diets of the many tribes, Zulus, Sotho and Xhosa, to name a few, and Colonial English, Dutch Afrikaner, India and Asia. So diverse is the food culture, it has been called the 'Rainbow Cuisine'. South Africans love their meat and aided by a sunny climate conducive to outdoor living, the South African BBQ or 'braai' is the everyday way of life. For the white South African, it is a constant whirl of eating, socializing and partying. The Internet was not even a twinkle in the eye, there was no downloading a recipe. The Housewives' League of South Africa Cookery Book became my personal chef, introducing me to traditional African dishes, vegetables and fruits new to me. I still have my Housewives' League of South Africa Cookery Book, published in 1967, 2nd edition printed in 1978.

> **Recipe titles from the Housewives' League of South Africa Cookery Book.**
> Krmeskies,
> Cream of Mealie Meal Soup,
> Fish Bobotie,
> Sea Eggs
> Pilchard Kedgeree,
> KingKlip Souffle,
> Gesmoorde Snoek,
> Panick Stations Stew,
> Banana Meat Loaf,
> Bahmi Goreng
> Saunders Old English Pie,
> Leg of Mutton Bengal Style,
> Marinated and Stewed Rabbit,
> Monkey Gland Steak,
> T-Bone Steaks with a Difference
> Boerewors Pie

Of the many dishes common to South Africa, bobotie with raisins, baked egg on top, is perhaps closest to a national dish because it is not made in any other country. A house-wife told me to add curry powder to get a slight tang. Much like our chewing gum, South Africans chew biltong – a stick of dried, cured meat. Boerewors is a sausage that is traditionally braaied. Ostrich farms abound and braaied ostrich steaks are delicious.

BOBOTIE

1 lb mincemeat	1 Tbs curry powder	1 tsp sugar
1 thick slice of bread	2 Eggs	1 cup of milk
1 onion	1 Tbs lemon juice	Salt and Pepper

Soak bread in milk. After 15 minutes, strain. Mash bread and add to mince. Add grated onion. Mix curry. Make custard by mixing the beaten eggs with the milk. Combine half this mixture with the meat. Place the meat in a greased pie dish and cover with remainder of custard. Top with dabs of butter, bake at 350F (180C) for 30 minutes.

Vegetables are very different in tropical climates. Waterblommetjie – practice saying it – is a water onion indigenous to South Africa particularly the Western Cape. It has a sweet-smelling flower and can be made into a bredie or stew or chopped fresh into salads. Waterblommetjie also makes a delicious vegetarian meal steamed and served with lemon aioli sauce and crusty bread or stirred into a risotto with chopped chilies. In the 1970s, pumpkin and other types of squash were not to be found in British stores. Spaghetti squash with its fibrous stringy interior is a delightful vegetable but I think pumpkin is, as they say, an acquired taste. Marmite I am told is also an acquired taste. Only Aussies and Brits seem to like it. I have found folks who do not like Marmite do not like pumpkin and those that like Marmite do not eat pumpkin. In Canada, pumpkin is a dessert as well as a vegetable. Yikes! Types of fruits not on British shelves in the 1970s were papaya, guava, granadilla, naartjies, pomegranate, paw-paw and spanspek.

The White Man's Burden

South Africans come over as chipper and very positive, sometimes a little arrogant. I could have well let myself take umbrage had I not stopped to think it was an inherent Boer temperament, just their way, nothing more. They are respectful to their elders and are madly principled about rules. The South African way of life is a disciplined one. Yet, they speak their mind and love to party. Sport is central to everything, rugby especially and they have an extraordinary sense of nationalism. With a wicked sense of humor, they have a mindset for the practical joke, love to wind each other up and everyone else too. The man of the house is 'da boss' the woman somewhat acquiescent, a good hostess and a stylish dresser. This is how I found it way back in 1978/9. I have to think that now it is very different. I have to think democracy has enabled and inspired South Africans black and white, to be their own person.

When you move to another country, there is the "lingo" to understand. When I first came to Canada, people would say to me, "See you later" and I thought *how friendly these Canadians are, so lovely to know we will be meeting again soon.* The reality is "See you later" is Canadianese for a firm "Goodbye" and there is no implied appointment.

In South Africa, the local lingo is a mixture of Afrikaans, Yiddish, English, and any one of the eleven tribal languages.

Running shoes were "takkies," not sneakers, track or gym shoes.

South Africans 'lekker' this or 'lekker' that. It is a much used word implying the speaker finds something nice, great, cool, or tasty. "That was a lekker braai!"

The English influence can be seen in words as 'nappy' not diaper as in North America and, again, in 'rubbish bin' not garbage bin.

South Africans use 'shame' frequently. It denotes they are feeling empathetic to you or to something. 'Shame man, don't you want to take some muti (medicine) for that babelaas (hangover)?' A South African admiring a baby or puppy, might say, Ag shame" to emphasize its cuteness. When in doubt, just say "Ag shame" and your sentiment will be greatly appreciated.

Many sentences are preceded with an "eish" or "ag" when there is an element of surprise or frustration, "Eish, the maid didn't come today" or an "ag" pronounced 'agh' to express irritation, "Ag man, what you do that for?"

In England, a truck is a lorry, in Canada, a 'pickup', in South Africa it is a 'bakkie.'

'Fixed up' is used to imply an arrangement is complete and the anticipated reply is, 'fixed up.'

Traffic lights are 'robots.'

'Bredies' are meat or vegetable stews.

A South African will tell you the house you are looking for is over the 'koppie' or hill.

"What's potting?" – What's up? This term has no gardening connotation whatsoever.

The White Man's Burden

Canada has Newfie jokes, Ireland has Pat and Mike jokes, Australia has Kiwi jokes and South Africa has Van der Merwe jokes. Van der Merwe is the iconic idiot Afrikaner. It is a common South African name much as Jones and Smith are common UK names. Jokes in the name of Van der Merwe cut across all divides ranging from the patently inane to cutting satire on Afrikaners' sexuality and politics. Afrikaners tell Van der Merwe jokes about themselves without feeling they are the direct butt of the jokes. They ranged from one-liners to dirty jokes, shaggy dog stories and tales that can be told for as long as you have the patience to listen. Humor ages and, reportedly, millennials do not find the humor funny.

"When Mr. Van der Merwe was given a dictionary for his birthday he confessed later that he could not follow the story but at least each word was explained as you went along."

"Here lays a great politician and an honest man," read the inscription on the gravestone. "Amazing," said Van de Merwe, "I never knew they put two oldies in one grave."

"The doctor talks to Van de Merwe's wife in the waiting room, "It's an ugly thing, Madam," he says. "Yes I know Doctor," she says, "but he's good with the children."

"Van de Merwe took his blond wife to a comedy show where they sat listening to comedians making one blond joke after another. The next act was a ventriloquist who also made blond jokes with a puppet on his lap. At this stage, Van de Merwe's wife was starting to fume and shouted out: "I'm sick and tired of you people treating blonds like idiots. I'll have you know

The White Man's Burden

I'm a quantum physics professor at the University of Cape Town." The ventriloquist became embarrassed and apologized to Mrs. Van de Merwe. She replied: "I wasn't talking to you. I'm talking to that dude on your lap!!!"

"Why did Van der Merwe keep a pair of scissors in his racing car? So he could cut corners."

In the midst of a transformed, democratic South Africa is a unique spot. It is a small town in the Northern Cape called Orania, a place white Afrikaners have created as a haven entirely for their own. In Orania, a black man will not be seen. Orania is the crown jewel to preserve the Afrikaner way of life. But there are differences to the Apartheid era when the white man reigned supreme. In Orania, there is no black man to do the manual and domestic jobs; white South Afrikaners do the man-about-the-house jobs, are the gardeners, garbage men, even gas attendants. Otherwise, it is all that the Afrikaner stood for in his heyday – church, non-intermarriage, discipline, order. Orania preserves its way of life while the outside world passes by. The residents of Orania safeguard their history with their own town holidays, run their own businesses and crime is virtually non-existent. It is an Afrikaner-only town where only Afrikaans is spoken. Orania is a town for those Afrikaners to feel they belong and to not feel deposed from a land they governed for many decades. Any white South African who claims white Afrikaner heritage is welcomed. In Orania, they feel inclusion and the safety of being white. There are, though, some breakthroughs in perspective. They dismiss the practices of Petit Apartheid, "You use that toilet, I use this toilet" as too extreme and unnecessary. The Government does not interfere in any way with this town of one thousand or more. Outside of Orania, in the move to democracy, Afrikaner monuments have been removed, streets and towns re-named and Afrikaner heritage is at total risk.

A traditional custom in black South Africa is the use of proverbs. Proverbs are valued as a fountain of richness of thought, reason, wisdom and philosophy. South African black elders use proverbs frequently. It is a source of pride to know many proverbs and certainly to know more than the next elder. Proverbs are used to impart wisdom to the young, as a device for informal cognitive therapy, sexuality, faith, family conflict, heritage. The task of the elders is to ensure the message of the proverbs gets handed down from one generation to the next, to make the meaning of the proverbs understood by the younger generation. However, I cannot imagine saying to my son as he introduces his life partner: "the one who loves an unsightly person is the one who makes her beautiful!"

"When a King has good counselors, his reign is peaceful."

AFRICAN PROVERB

CHAPTER 10

"Oh the Places You'll Go."

– Dr. Seuss

South Africa, vast, beautiful, rugged, tree-dotted bushveld, wide open savanna, dense rain-forests, mountain ranges, long sandy beaches, massive surfing waves, the home of the lion, land of sun, exotic, enticing, and all within a day's drive of our home. Our desire to see as much as we could was voracious. I knew in my heart that we could never afford to return, that to have bananas growing in my garden, a lizard in the mailbox, giant toads in the pool, was well and truly the opportunity of our lifetime. That being said, we were not on vacation. We were here with Philip on work assignment with a limited time in which to do it and our opportunity for travel was restricted to days he could take off work. We also had children in school and a toddler. Expectations are different when children are involved; places have to be child friendly and child interesting.

We snatched as many holiday weeks and long weekends as we could and took advantage of statutory holidays. It was to our advantage that the children had an inordinate number of days off school for name days, Ascension Day, Republic Day, Settlers Day, Kruger Day, the Day of the Covenant, Van Riebeeck's Day, Founder's Day, Family Day apart from the standard holidays of Christmas and Easter. It was a whole new experience to have Santa and the Christmas break in blazing hot sun. I scoured food stores to buy a turkey for Christmas Day but South Africa, at least in the Johannesburg area at that time, seemed to know nothing of turkeys. We could have had ostrich meat or bison but of turkey – nothing. I did find a brandy plum Christmas pudding at Marks and Spencer. That year, we had a very different Christmas, fillet steaks, sausage on the 'braai' and flamed the Christmas pudding holding it high in the swimming pool.

Tourists proposing to come to Vancouver, Canada, for two weeks would say: "I've done Canada." And I would reply: "To *do* Canada is weeks of driving or making multiple air flights. My brother telephoned about his upcoming visit to Canada. "From Vancouver, I'll drive over to Victoria Sunday afternoon," he said.

> "David, you can swim to Victoria or catch the ferry across the thirty-two kilometers of ocean but there is no road between Vancouver and Victoria."
> "That would be the Atlantic ocean?"
> "No, the North Pacific."

Like Canada, South Africa is a country of air flights or long, very long, car drives.

One evening, we prioritized the places we felt we just had to see before we left and came up with the following list:

The White Man's Burden

- ✔ Soweto, the black township
- ✔ Pretoria
- ✔ The Kruger National Park
- ✔ Durban, Natal
- ✔ Zululand – the Three Rondavels and God's Window
- ✔ Cape Town, Table Mountain

Black South Africans have incredible language skills and can switch from one tribal language to another, Zulu to Xhosa to Sotho and more and also to Afrikaans and English. Mainstream South African English is littered with words and phrases from tribal languages such as Sawubona, Zulu for hello, Usana, Xhosa for baby.

Soweto was twenty miles south-west of Johannesburg, forty minutes' drive from Kensington B. The name, 'Soweto' conjures up an African name but the word is formed from an acronym for 'SOuth WEstern TOwnships.' To name the township, there was a four-year long public competition. Goes without saying, it was a whites-only vote. It brings to mind a similar public naming competition in Toronto when the voters were overwhelmingly black. The new name was the Toronto Raptors.

If I were black in those times, I might well have spat out a few unpublishable words or even hurled a brick or two at a white passerby. The message was it was unsafe for whites to drive privately into Soweto. We obtained official entry passes and toured on an official bus with a white tour guide. We took the tour while the children were in school and left Elizabeth with Rosemary.

We had some discussion about whether taking the older children to Soweto would be an educational experience for them. It meant missing a morning's school but there was only one opportunity. They would be interested if the tour was a real look into Soweto but our thoughts were it was a good publicity setup for tourists – and we were right.

On each seat in the bus was a pamphlet from the South African Department of Information about South Africa's township policies, a rebuttal to the world criticism that the National Government considered unfounded. The pamphlet read that those familiar with other African cities would know Soweto to be high-class living. The Preface in the Soweto tourist bus handout read:

> *"Conveniently, for South Africa's detractors and vilifiers, the name of the country's largest Black city, Soweto, happens to rhyme with the word "ghetto." Once they've said, "Soweto is a ghetto," there is nothing more to say. "Don't let the facts stand in the way of a good story" is an adage well known to media people the world over and, unfortunately, too many freely avail themselves of it."*

The bus drove passed rows and rows of identical matchbox houses their corrugated iron roofs receding into the distance as far as the eye could see. Each house had a small plot of garden. The tour guide pointed to the Mayor's house, rather fancier, a modern bungalow of plaster construction, a tiled roof amid a nicely landscaped garden. I was set to see a disheveled shantytown and was expecting much worse. Plain as the houses were, I could in no way describe them as disheveled. The little boxes were prettily painted, the gardens neatly weeded with colorful flowers in border beds.

The White Man's Burden

There seemed to be an obvious effort by Sowetans to keep their modest dwellings looking fresh. The expression house-proud came to mind. The picturesque, cute homes came over to me as contrived, kind of like a film set, unreal. I wondered if the bus was avoiding darker, poorer slum areas, unserviced shacks. To be honest, I could have agreed with the pamphlet that the housing was adequate if the black occupants of those Soweto houses had voting rights, free education, medical services, social security, electricity and running water. Rather than one atop another as are low income high-rise apartments in Toronto and Vancouver, the matchbox houses were built side-by-side. Space management becomes an issue in cities. Nevertheless, to have a private front door opening to the street and a little garden is homely and quite priceless.

We saw signs of community living – the butcher, baker, grocer, fruit and vegetables shop, churches, the Afribank (a black-controlled bank), a movie house, sports arena, many unkempt playing fields. There were no indications of industry, manufacturing or building although we passed by numerous 'shebeens' – beer halls.

The guide told us the infant mortality rate in Soweto was high. He put it down to the smoke from coal used for cooking and heating that affects the breathing of Sowetan babies. Public transport was sparse and the few taxis we saw seemed to be packed. A cushy business", said the guide, "to own a taxi". Newspapers reported it was not cheap to shop in this township of all momma-poppa businesses. The owners were unable to buy in bulk as do supermarkets and had no alternative but to pass on the markup to customers. The paradox was the people with the lowest incomes were paying the highest prices.

The White Man's Burden

Sowetans still lived the African way, simply, the coal stove and the washboard. White businessmen were quick to see the potential for money making big time. In the two years we were in South Africa, we watched the change happen. The newspapers and television commercials portrayed smiley black housewives drooling over their newly acquired washing machines, refrigerators and vacuum cleaners. For this, electricity had to be available and parts of Soweto were targeted for power supply.

The tour bus stopped at the Witch Doctor's house. The African word for Witch Doctor is 'Sangoma' but a true Sangoma is more a naturopath than a Witch Doctor, skilled in the use of herbs and roots. Sangomas distanced themselves from Witch Doctors, whom they said gave the profession a bad name casting evil spells and claiming to be able to see beyond the human world. A long line of people waited for 'consultations' with the Witch Doctor who was secluded behind a curtained fenced yard where hung skulls, seed pods, feathers, weird figurines, carvings and other mysterious items of unknown origin. Much credence is given to the insights Witch Doctors have into the spirit world and their ability to communicate with the dead. "A consultation," I thought, "why not?" A tall black woman, made the more so by a high hat, a long highly colored coat, triple rows of gold chains and beads about her neck, advised me that I had bad spirits coming from my mother's side and from my employer. Her solution was to talk to my mother's ancestors to ask them to back off and to quit my job; I handed her ten rand and reckoned she was on to a good thing!

Pretoria was next on our list about fifty-five kilometers from Johannesburg. Pretoria is the administrative capital for the civil service, government departments, Foreign Embassies and

High Commissioners. Cape Town is the legislative capital and Bloemfontein in the Orange Free State is the seat of justice.

In spring, Pretoria comes alive with purple blossoming Jacaranda trees lining its streets giving rise to its nickname, Jacaranda City. There is a superstition that should a blossom fall on to the head of a student at the University of Pretoria, he or she will pass with honors. Nelson Mandela in his book *Long Walk to Freedom*, remarks that during his treason trial, the accused were permitted to have lunch in a nearby garden: "Those moments under the shade of the Jacaranda trees on the vicarage lawn were the most pleasant of the trial …"

Pretoria was a pleasant city of old government offices and parks, not really a tourist town. It is also an academic city with three universities. The slow pace of life in Pretoria was the reason many workers preferred to commute to work rather than live in the comparative rat race of Johannesburg. Lately, there have been proposals to change the name of Pretoria to 'Tshwane' but the proposal was stalled; Pretoria is largely Afrikaans and, so far, nothing has changed.

The Voortrekker Monument is about the only must visit in Pretoria for the tourist. It is an imposing building that dwarfs the city for miles around. The Monument was built as a shrine to immortalize the courage and dedication of the Voortrekkers in their long trek from the Cape and eventual settlement in northeast South Africa. It is revered by Afrikaners as sacred, a sentiment conveyed in the notice at the entrance: 'Visitors must be suitably dressed; not allowed are ladies in shorts (tights); men in sleeveless shirts" by order, Board of Control'.

The White Man's Burden

It is a celestial experience to stand in the beam of sunlight that streams down from the dome of the Monument to directly pinpoint the words hundreds of feet below: 'Ons vir Jou, Suid-Afrika' (We for Thee, South Africa.). Inset into the outside walls of the Voortrekker monument are sixty-four sculpted horse-drawn wagons depicting the number of wagons at the Battle of Blood River, the final battle against Dingane, King of the Zulus. We discussed with the children the rights and wrongs of taking lands belonging to others which went off target to a discussion on 1066 when King Harold got an arrow in his eye, and England's crook-back King Richard the Third.

Outside the Memorial, a bronze sculpture of a Voortrekker mother and her two children pays homage to the strength and courage of the Voortrekker women. This sculpture is so absolutely huge that the photograph we took with our three children at its base miniaturizes them to the size of ants.

For a short time, there was petrol rationing in South Africa due to OPEC oil sanctions against Apartheid. South Africa converts coal to gasoline as well as to diesel fuel. Self-sufficient in petroleum, it defiantly responded it had enough oil reserves to last many years and threatened to cut off the export of diamonds if the gas restrictions were not lifted. The diamond threat was taken extremely seriously and, as expected, the oil embargo did not last long. Rationing on gasoline permitted only travel to work and back; there was no allowance for holidays or personal trips. Tourists, a large part of South Africa's economy, were exempted from gas rationing. There is a fine delineation between temporary residents and tourists but some wheeling and dealing at government level had us classified as tourists and exempted from gas restrictions.

Even so, for each road trip we wished to make, we had to apply for an 'After Hours Refueling Permit.'

> 'Permit #03/D-93627, 12th January, 1979
>
> Tourist, passport #557263M
>
> Purpose for which required:
>
> Authority is hereby given to Mr. P. A. Bogod of 29 Victoria Street, Kensington B, Randburg, to purchase fuel during the period 22nd February 1979 to 28th February 1979 outside prescribed hours at any service station for use with registration TJ 156/792 on the following route in the Republic of South Africa.
>
> Authority is also hereby granted for service stations on the above route to supply fuel during the above-mentioned authorized period direct into the tank of the above-mentioned vehicle.
>
> Full signature of Issuing Office and Official: Date Stamp, 25th January 1979, Magistrate's Office. This Permit is not valid unless it bears the official date stamp of the issuing officer. This Authority may be withdrawn at any time with- out prior notice.'

(The above was also translated into Afrikaans.)

The opportunity to open eyes to new ways, experience different cultures, diversity of peoples and see animals in the wild were the reasons I had readily agreed for the children to have four months off their school in England, which said four months lengthened to two years. We could not leave South Africa without a visit to a Game Reserve to experience the wonder of animals in their natural habitat.

The Kruger National Park was the premier Nature Reserve in South Africa. We took a name-day holiday weekend to make the journey, anti-malaria tablets at the ready. It was a long drive, about six hours. We passed fields of sugar cane, orange and grapefruit trees and stopped at the small farming city of Nelspruit for dinner. Then, it was all-systems-go to the Paul Kruger Gate, one of several entrances to the Kruger National Park. In the 1970s, tour buses or safari land rovers were not the mode of transport in the Kruger National Park. Visitors drove through the park in their private cars. At the entry gate, the gate keeper warned, "Keep the windows closed."

Today, the Kruger National Park is preserved as a national heritage park – open-top tour buses with guides proliferate as do luxury safari lodges, digital cameras, spas and sumptuous hotels. Afternoon tea is served before the evening game drive.

We had been driving for two hours and seen nothing. The children were getting antsy and so was I. *Was this a Nature Reserve or had we been tricked?* It was our ever-observant daughter Karen who, overcome with excitement, wagging an index finger at the window, spluttered, "There, over there." We all looked as hard as we could but none of us had her keen eyes. Then we saw what she was seeing, the shadowy rows of tall necks trailing each other, tall as the trees they followed. We were looking at giraffe. For a perfect example of camouflage, have a look at the photograph in this book to see why we had such difficulty spotting giraffe. After sighting giraffe, the tension in the car was palpable. Round every corner, we anticipated animals but there were none. The expectation of jungle animals at any minute kept all eyes glued to the windows and two hour gaps between sightings passed as minutes. Round any corner there could be something bold, something fierce or giant. Our patience was finally rewarded with herds of zebra, rhino, leopards, wildebeest, impala and particularly the hyena that passed right in front of our car, its dinner in its mouth.

We stopped that night in a kraal, an African village. Within the kraal were rondavels, oval houses constructed of mortar mixed with soil and cow dung. Each rondavel had a thatched roof tapering to a point. As we settled for bed, it was eerie and somewhat disconcerting to hear the baying and howling of wild beasts roaming the night free and close-by yet we knew we were safe because an electric fence surrounded the kraal. Inside our rondavel it was camp-style with five cots. There were outhouse toilets and a rondavel community kitchen. In the morning, we had breakfast in the kitchen – bacon, eggs, toast and marmalade, juice and coffee – an English breakfast, couldn't be better.

The second day, we crossed a small river by a bridge beneath which lay lazy, satiated crocodiles idling in the sun. Even in sleep, they looked fearsome and I was glad to have the bridge between us. At the turn of the road, we encountered head on a huge African elephant. We had been told if we met elephant, we should put the car slowly into reverse. Elephant can be aggressive in season if they are protecting their young. The elephant seemed to be by itself but we knew there had to be others close by. The children were terrified and screaming and me too. Philip kept his cool and slowly backed up the car. The huge animal, twice the height of our car, slowly lumbered by, unfazed.

The White Man's Burden

If you are on safari in Africa and spot a tiger, I regret you caught the wrong airplane – tigers live in India. I was sorely disappointed we did not see any lions. A trip to the Kruger Park is not like visiting a zoo where you buy a zoo map and systematically plan your route to see all the animals. In the Kruger Park, you have to take what nature offers when and where, and encounters are luck, hit and miss. However, all told, the Kruger National Park in the presence of both prey and predator is unforgettable. There is nothing to equal animals in their natural habitat, knowing they are not fed from buckets, and to witness so dramatically the sequence of life. A visit to an African National Park strengthens respect and deepens kinship with living things, reminds us of our place in evolution. It makes visits to zoos and theme parks a tame experience. I have been spoiled and I am not above bragging.

I had thought a visit to Johannesburg Zoo should be worthwhile; after all, this was Africa the home of the jungle beasts. I took Elizabeth while the older children were at school. I thought a zoo in South Africa's major city would be spectacular. My expectations were high and I was in for a letdown. The Johannesburg Zoo in 1979 was a dismal affair, grey overall, small enclosures, concrete squares. As a child in England, I had visited Whipsnade Zoo, a zoo enlightened beyond its time. Its setting was open countryside; its animals of the jungle though not free, were able to roam treed areas so large it was often difficult to spot the inhabitants. Bounded by electric fences, visitors drove the intersecting roads and stopped to take closer looks. It was not the wild, natural habitat of the Kruger National Park but it was a very good attempt.

Back then, black South Africans had to apply for a permit to visit the Johannesburg Zoo. I believe today, the Johannesburg

Zoo has had a makeover so forget all the above. When you are in Jo'burg, make a visit to the zoo. I am sure you will be well rewarded.

From Johannesburg to the Cape by the Garden Route is eighteen hundred miles, a week's drive and that only if there is no stop for water, toilets, car sickness or back-seat fights. People we spoke to raved about the beautiful drive to Cape Town, the beaches, forests, desert and wildlife. Dearly, we would have loved to have traveled the Garden Route to Cape Town, but in practical terms, with kids and limited time, it was not a viable plan. I heard conflicting views on the scenic value of the Garden Route ranging from "You can see oceans one side and green mountains on the other" to "In truth, it's a nice road, but nothing else." Either way, the choice for us was already made. It was air from Johannesburg to Cape Town.

Off the southwestern tip of the country is the Cape of Good Hope. My memory shot back to school history, the great explorers, Vasco Da Gama and Bartolomeo Dias, the omnipotent power of the sea, the galleons, sails unfurled bestriding treacherous waves, many floundering as they rounded the Cape, a sailor's nightmare; land, ahoy up the mainsail!

Our time at Table Mountain was somewhat restricted because we had in tow our plump, heavy, eighteen-month daughter, diaper bag, stroller and other toddler accoutrements. For us there was no rock climbing or trekking up the mountain, but the five-minute cable car. As the cable car slowly lurched up the mountain, through the glass cage windows we could see the young and unencumbered souls who reached the top the physical way. We watched carefully placed footholds and cautious grips on the rocky boulders. I was so glad to have an excuse to use the cable car.

Table Mountain was clothed in the white clouds known locally as the 'table cloth'. I have to confess to some disappointment with Table Mountain. I am a lover of mountains and, in their presence, feel the awesome power of their height and range. When I die, I would like my ashes spread in the mountains. However, the mountains that I love are steep, vast, towering peaks and valleys, ridges and gorges as are the Rockies and the Alps. And this one was flat!

The kids heard that the Indian Ocean and the Atlantic Ocean somehow collide at Cape Town. It made for a good story and a way to busy them in an exercise of imaginative impossibility, to jump from the warm Indian water into the cold Cape Town water. That these two oceans abut is a myth but a myth with a grain of truth. On the southern shoreline, the two oceans do meet but there is the Cape Peninsula in between. Generally, the water at the Cape is cold, but with southeasterly and northwesterly winds, the warm current of the Indian Ocean can drift as far as Cape Town to make the waters warmer.

The pageantry of the open-air market in Cape Town was vibrant, colorful, noisy and fun, a hard to resist lure for buying souvenirs and gifts. The many open market stalls were a miscellany of traditional African prints, tribal masks, hand-painted pottery, beaded bottles, African dolls, carved wooden witch doctors, tapestries and baskets in all shapes and sizes. There were throngs of tourists eager to buy and vendors eager to sell, an ambience of tradition and custom. Uncertain whether 'haggling' was the practice, we stood by and watched as scenes of negotiation became perceived bargains. I am sufficiently skeptical to believe all was an act and that the sellers always got the deals they were expecting.

In our time in South Africa, Camps Bay beach was opened to all races and overcrowding became a problem. It got so serious that Camps Bay rate-payers held a referendum to decide whether the beach should remain open to all races and voters overwhelmingly decided the beach was for all races. The crowds that ensued made for much drinking and unruly behavior causing the municipality to re-think its policy. It came up with a strategy to install a fence dividing the beach and to charge entry to one side. It was a no-brainer on the outcome, the sunbathers and swimmers all crowded into the free side, the fee-paying side remaining empty. The fence was removed.

The day we visited Camps Bay beach, 'multi-racial' was a misnomer because the beach was completely deserted of black white or any color, just the five of us. Camps Bay is a paradise setting in a beautiful cove, rolling and crashing waves resolving into crystal-clear water lapping the white soft sands. Framed by the backdrop of the Twelve Apostles Mountains and the towering peak of the Lion's Head, it is, undoubtedly, the most beautiful beach I have seen. What is more, we had this glorious beach all to ourselves. Unable to fit the Twelve Apostles into the scope of his camera, Philip took three shots, each with four Apostles, the idea to physically paste the three photos together in our yet to be developed scrapbook. The kids were eager to wade into the breaking waves. Swimming in the English Channel is quite cold but they found the Atlantic at Camps Bay too cold to even paddle at the water's edge. I pointed to the warning notice on the beach,

The White Man's Burden

"Offshore nets are provided but all persons entering the sea do so at their own risk. Avoid bathing at dawn, dusk and at night when SHARK attack is more likely."

The warning served its purpose to scare them and they were more than content to play in the many rock pools with crabs and small fish and at the children's playground.

The sanctions imposed in London on South Africa included the sale of South African wine and we wanted to treat ourselves to a case of South African wines not to take back to the UK but to consume while in South Africa. The area of Stellenbosch, a forty-five kilometer drive from Cape Town is renowned for its twenty-two wineries. The proverbial rules were on display and we actually agreed on one rule – no alcohol for the children. The Wine Farm provided grape juice for the children who felt very grown-up when asked to choose red, white or rosé. There was an activity sheet for children about the role that insects play in the vineyard, good and bad. It seems it is constant war on bugs in the vineyard. The vine-mealy bugs eat the vine leaf and a bottle of Sauvignon Blanc can pick up the flavor of leaf-eating ants! There was a park at the side of a lake which made a lovely setting for a picnic. Packed picnics could be bought – platters of cheese, pâté paired with wines and, of course, grapes. In the mini-zoo, we held eagles and owls, touched gymogenes (striped birds of prey) while screeching monkeys leapt tree to tree.

In Cape Town, we saw the outside of the Groote Schuur Hospital. Not just another hospital, Groote Schuur has a very special meaning. The first human heart transplant took place at this hospital in 1967 performed by Dr. Christiaan Barnard and the recipient was Louis Washkansky, a fifty three year old grocer. In the workup to the final operation, Chris Barnard used the hearts of male chimps. "As we put the chimp to sleep in his cage in preparation for the operation, he chattered and cried incessantly. We attached no significance to this, but it must have made a great impression on his companion for when we removed the body to the operating room, the other chimp wept bitterly and was inconsolable for days." Dr. Barnard was also heard to say that, if he could have used a black man's heart, the operation could have been performed two weeks earlier.

During the Christmas school holidays, we were invited to a three-week camp in Margate, Natal. It was midsummer and very hot. Many South Africans take the opportunity to have a vacation at this time of year. We slept in bunk houses and ate communally in the big bunk house. Friends with babies and toddlers going to the camp were taking their maid. We, too, had a baby, so we asked Rosemary if she would like to nanny for us. Maids had to sleep in maids' tents not in the bunk house we occupied. It was not sleeping in a tent that was Rosemary's problem. The problem was that Rosemary was Zulu and the maids in the tent were Xhosa. Rosemary came to me next day to ask for a change of tent with Zulu inhabitants. We talked to camp management and were able to change her sleeping quarters. In a nation where automatically white man versus black man comes to mind, there was a whole other set of problems – infighting quarrels and feuds between the different tribes. Zulu is the largest tribe in South Africa and its roots are in the province of Natal, today known as KwaZulu-Natal. The Xhosa primarily inhabit the Homelands of Transkei and Ciskei, now known as the Eastern Cape.

We spent several lazy, hazy days in paradise on Umhlanga Beach near Durban. It is a postcard beach, a curved cove with soft white sand and the rolling waves of the warm waters of the Indian Ocean. It was, of course, an all-whites beach. My fondest memory of Umhlanga Beach is that it was those far off days when I looked good in a bikini!

Purely by chance, Nicholas encountered his school friend, Ralph, on the beach. Having only the company of two sisters, boy company was just what he needed. The two boys had tremendous fun in and out of the Indian Ocean, jumping the huge rolling waves, consuming delicious and cooling ice cream sodas from the beach vendors. Unfortunately, sunburn caught Nicholas. While sunburn is nothing unusual among tourists at Umhlanga, the Natal sun can be brutal and Nicholas woke next morning, his eyes virtually closed his face swollen and painful. It put paid to next day on the beach. The camp doctor prescribed a curing cream and all was back to normal in a couple of days.

"A white child, deeply sun-burnt after a month's holiday at Muizenberg, was ordered out of a "net wittes" coach by a train conductor this week."

Argus, January 14, 1956

The Valley of a Thousand Hills between Pietermaritzburg and Durban was a panorama of endless undulating green, velvet rolling hills and forests. Here was a tourist replica of a Zulu village with kraals, farms and the inevitable witch doctor. The near-naked Zulu ladies at the Village earned themselves a respectable living educating tourists about Zulu culture and performing traditional Zulu dances. They were overly eager to pose for photographs and tips. Karen, Elizabeth and I joined the Zulu ladies for a group

The White Man's Burden

photo but it was all too much for our Nicholas at age eleven. "There is no way," he said, "I am going to stand amongst those boobs."

We went touristy berserk buying Zulu souvenirs. We bought a Transvaal tapestry rug depicting warriors fighting with spears, woven blood dripping down the canvas. Today, the tapestry hangs on our living room wall. Also among our buys was a beautiful soap-stone chess set, its King, a Zulu king, its Queen, a Zulu queen, witch doctor Bishops, Zulu warrior Knights, kraals as Castles and Zulu tribesmen as Pawns. Sadly on our journeys, this chess set was lost despite each piece being individually wrapped in tissue paper and all boxed. We also bought a glass liqueur bottle encased in interwoven beads of red, blue, orange and green, two pottery kraals painted with traditional African designs, two Zulu clothes-peg warriors with spears and straw skirts. In a secure corner of our Canadian home heavily encased in newspaper, rests the deadly Zulu spear with its accompanying bow and arrows. As good tourists, we had to think about gifts to give to the folks on our return. We bought several sets of African teak salad servers, the handles of each carved as giraffe or impala.

I wondered about the inspiration to call a land-feature 'God's Window' and hoped it lived up to its name. It did. From the cliff top, it is a sheer drop of 2,500 feet down to the four miles of the plains of the South African lowveld with the Kruger National Park in the far distance. From so high to so low, it takes on an 'Eden' appearance and I felt the visceral experience that prompted its name. God's Window features prominently in the 1980s South African cult film 'The Gods Must Be Crazy'. Near the end of the movie, the Bushman character Xi (played by Namibian bush farmer N!xau) travels to God's Window, and due to low-lying cloud cover, believes it to be the end of the Earth.

The White Man's Burden

A short drive from God's Window was the third of the three tourist spots on our list: the Three Rondavels, gigantic peaks shaped like the traditional rondavels of the African tribes. The three peaks colloquially personified as The Three Sisters. These sisters were the troublesome wives of Chief Maripi Mashile who routed invading warriors from Swaziland in a great battle and whose name has lived on as 'The very great one.' The three wives from right to left are named Maseroto, Mogoladikwe and Magabolle. For the kids in the back seat of the car, a story of spears, shields and blood made a welcome diversion especially since it took a while between initially sighting to actually passing the Three Rondavels. On the long drive from Johannesburg to Durban, the majestic Drakensburg Mountains loomed like a trusted guardian ever on guard.

There were roadside picnic tables for the convenience of picnickers on most South African highways. The children always had countless needs for roadside stops to stretch legs or for toilet facilities so we welcomed these table stops. We stopped to eat a lunch I had brought of sandwiches, fruit and cake. After we had eaten, we emptied the leftovers into a garbage container. South Africa is very particular about tidiness and cleanliness and provided many very helpful waste containers in obscure places around the countryside. Back in the car as we started off to resume our journey, through the rear back window we saw three small black children emerge, very cautiously, from the bush. They were out to grab any scraps we had left on the picnic table. We had been careful to clear the table and discard our rubbish so there was really nothing left other than crumbs. I mentioned to the children that we still had half a cake left in the boot which we did not need and we could leave it on the table. This idea was met with great enthusiasm. We reversed the car a tad, opened the boot and Nicholas jumped out to set the half-cake on the picnic table. Through the car rear window as we drove away, we saw three black children emerge from the bush to grab what we had put on the picnic table. We were immensely moved by the experience, especially the children who had a real life dose of how it is to be black and hungry in South Africa.

On the long drive back from Durban to Johannesburg we were hailed by a black South African wildly gesticulating for us to stop. We assumed he was a hitchhiker. These were the days before everybody was deemed to be a kidnapper and hitch-hikers were considered to be legitimate adventurous travelers without transport wishing to get somewhere near their destination. It was an entirely deserted road and we stopped. Apparently, he did not want a ride. He pointed back down the long empty road uttering a stream of Zulu. Puzzled, all became clear when we saw the roof rack atop our car with a large empty gap. A suitcase had detached itself from its bindings and fallen off on to the road. It had to be close on the highway somewhere because this helpful man had seen it drop. We thanked him as best we could and reversed the car back to try to locate the suitcase. We looked hard, very hard. All the kids got out and even the keen-eyed Karen could not find the suitcase. There was no sign of it anywhere. It seemed somebody had got a good haul in the short time between our dropping the case and going back to retrieve it. Not only did the suitcase contain clothing but it also contained an envelope with five-hundred rand, the next payment of our rent. Fortunately, our cash was insured and we were not the losers. In an area of massive poverty and unemployment, we could only have empathy for the quick-footed thief who had been clever enough to make himself a year's income in five minutes.

Our coveted 1 oz of gold – a Krugerrand

Nicholas at the Snake Park, Johannesburg, with a poisonous mamba

Nicholas in his bean bag

Nicholas and Karen with two mine dancers, Johannesburg

Rosemary and Elizabeth

In the Kruger National Park, "I saw elephant!"

Philip and Alex, the guard dog who shook like a jelly in a thunderstorm

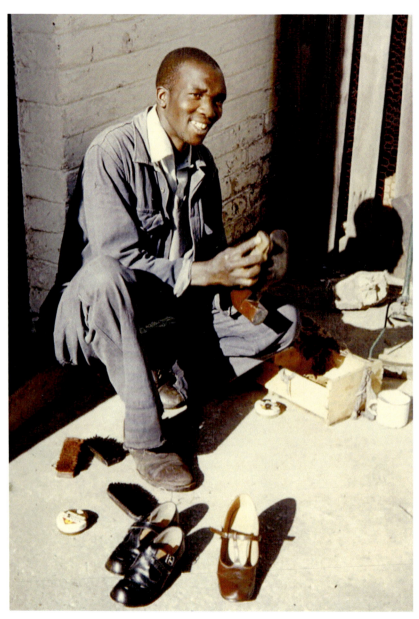
Philemon polishing the family's shoes

Find the giraffe

Woman and Children Statue Voortrekker Monument, Pretoria so large it dwarfs Nicholas, Karen and Elizabeth at its base

Umhlanga Beach, near Durban, Natal. Karen, Nicholas and me in a bikini!

Valley of a Thousand Hills, Zululand, Natal
Karen, Elizabeth and me

Protea – South Africa's National Flower

Strelitzia – like a bird of paradise

The package in the mailbox

Elizabeth and the baby ostriches
"You're so cute."
"So are you."

Rosemary's house outside Pietersburg, Transvaal

Soweto, 1979

Karen in the atrium with a bunch of bananas

CHAPTER 11

A Lonely Little Petunia in an Onion Patch

1997 – Robben Island, Cape Town, South Africa

"No one is born hating another person because of the color of his skin, or his background, or his religion. People must learn to hate, and if they can learn to hate, they can be taught to love, for love comes more naturally to the human heart than its opposite."

NELSON MANDELA

From the top of Table Mountain, I could see a blip in the ocean, a split from the mainland, a volcanic eruption from the earth's core. The little mound seemed oddly out of place by itself and brought to mind the kids' song, 'I'm a lonely little petunia in an onion patch'. Table Mountain is a mecca for all tourists visiting Cape Town for the spectacular view from its top of the Atlantic Ocean. The blip in the ocean was Robben Island. That I was so close to Inmate 46664 yet so far, even now sends shivers through my spine.

In 2017, there are few who have not heard of Nelson Mandela and do not associate him as the savior of South Africa's black population, a nation battered by racial intolerance. Standing atop that mountain, neither I nor anyone could have imagined that there among the many inmates on that tiny island dwelled the man who brought about this miracle and did so without bloodshed.

Nelson Mandela was forty-four when he was sentenced for treason and seventy-one when he was released. A question that puzzles many is how is it possible to be deprived of freedom for so many years yet emerge so free of hate, resentment and revenge so much so that retaliation by physical payback was as abhorrent to him as the racial inequity which cost him his freedom. Nelson Mandela has, himself, supplied the answer, "Hating clouds the mind. It gets in the way of strategy. Leaders cannot afford to hate."

The cells on Robben Island were small and damp, so small that an inmate lying down could feel the far wall with his head and the opposite wall with his feet. There were mats and blankets, no running water, and sanitary buckets for toilets. Hard labor at Robben Island was in a lime quarry, back-breaking work hacking through rock with a pick, shovel and wheelbarrow. The levels of discipline at any time on Robben Island were dependent on the temperament of the guards of the day, a matter of luck. The more laid-back the officers, the more chatting. The more rigid the guards, the more quarrying. The occasional guard was approachable but mostly guards were unbending, inflexible. The prison guards became noticeably deferential during the few visits from the Red Cross. Red Cross visits did bring about some small improvements, for example long pants and socks badly needed for protection from the very hot sun.

Helen Suzman, a Member of the official opposition the Progressive Party, was a bug in the ears to the National Party's political rule for white supremacy. Mrs. Suzman paid many visits to Robben Island. On the first visit in 1967, she asked inmates if they had any complaints. The replies were, yes, they had many complaints but she should refer to Nelson Mandela, Inmate #46664, who would talk on their behalf. Even then it was apparent Mandela was a leader.

Moved to Pollsmoor Prison near Johannesburg for the talks about democracy, Nelson Mandela describes Pollsmore as "the prison's penthouse: a spacious room about fifty feet by thirty on the third and topmost floor of the prison, a separate section with a toilet, urinal, two basins, two showers and four proper beds as well as radio and newspapers. Compared with Robben Island, we were in a five-star hotel," he adds.

At his trial, Nelson Mandela spoke of white Afrikaners: "They do not look upon South African black peoples as people with families of their own. They do not realize that they have emotions; that they fall in love like white people do; that they want to be with their wives and children like white people want to be with their wives and children. They want to earn enough money to support their families properly, to feed and clothe them and send them to school, and what house-boy or garden-boy or laborer can ever hope to do this?"

The White Man's Burden

Brought to trial and convicted of high treason against the State, the penalty was death. At his sentencing Mandela said he was prepared to die for his fight against white supremacy. Some say it was those words spoken so fervently from his heart that saved him from the gallows; that the unthinkable happened, Nelson Mandela had pierced the Afrikaner heart. Others feel it was more likely a political decision. The Apartheid Government was well aware that black South Africans revered and venerated Nelson Mandela as a man larger than life itself. To the black South African, he was a leader and a hero. To execute him would have added fuel to an already boiling pot. In political terms, a martyr would not sit well in the public arena or add strength to the white South Afrikaner purpose. For these reasons, it was not politically savvy to execute him. I wonder would South Africa ever have found its way to democracy without this man.

After the Second World War, my father's brother, my Uncle Magnus, immigrated to Cape Town with his wife and two sons, Gordon and John. My uncle returned to London for our wedding in 1961. We two love-birds expressed an interest in South Africa. The country appealed to us with its warm climate and strong economy. Our suggestion was met with stern rebuke, "Over my dead body," said my uncle. Like many South Africans, my uncle believed civil war was a time bomb in waiting, a blood bath, to depose the Apartheid National Government.

As the world was yet to find, that was not the Mandela way. The transition to democracy was smooth and peaceful, not a shot fired. Madiba was the name of Mandela's clan, a name which came to signify respect and affection of black and white South Africans for this insightful, humble, freedom fighter, beloved for his courage, his leadership, his gentleness, his abhorrence of violence. He was a man who changed the course of history his way – with humanity and dignity.

I wonder about racism, why people get so het up over skin color, eye shapes, kinky hair; the belief that one race is inferior or superior to another. Babies are not born racist. It follows that racism must be a learned process. My four-month-old puppy had never seen a wheelchair. She reacted with fear to this new object. She is used to wheelchairs now, no longer fears them and accepts them as a regular feature of her daily walks. Were we to see a man with black skin for the first time, we would likely run. The flight or fight response is innate to us all, animal or human. In our formative years, if we are taught about 'difference,' ethnic diversity, and how all major religions share the common goal of love, tolerance and forgiveness, we too would accept these differences as regular features of our daily walks, just as my puppy does.

Among free-thinkers, how many of us can honestly say we are not just a little racist? Doesn't racism lurk deep within us all but is hard to admit, not politically correct? How shameful to announce publicly or even privately that one would prefer to have a white daughter in-law.

Most would say a racist is the product of prejudiced parents, a neglected kid, sternly and rigidly raised. No dad and son kicked a ball round the park; no father tousled his hair, told him it was okay to cry; no mother sensitive to her child's transition into manhood, his wondering, questioning, seeking and his yearning for praise while still counting on a cuddle. The now drifting adult comes to know anger, envy, self-indulgence, but of achievement, fulfillment or purpose, he knows nothing. He cannot identify with a largely compassionate world and it helps to deflect his pain upon a scapegoat, an entity he sees as different, the black man. He feels the intoxication of his power. In the extreme degree, he is a tyrannical force. This is a racist.

As human beings, we herd into groups, social, ethnic, religious, popular, even 'alone' groups. We can be pressured into going with the winning team; we can be left navigating our way through the maze of values that is the complexity of life. If our own values are compromised, what hope is there for us to live in harmony and peace?

> "You've got to be taught to hate and fear.
> You've got to be taught from year to year.
> It's got to be drummed in your dear little ear,
> You've got to be carefully taught.
>
> You've got to be taught to be afraid
> Of people whose eyes are oddly made
> And people whose skin is a different shade,
> You've got to be carefully taught.
>
> "You've got to be taught before its too late,
> Before you are six or seven or eight,
> To hate all the people your relatives hate.
> You've got to be carefully taught.
> You've got to be carefully taught."

You've got to be carefully taught!
Oscar Hammerstein II, South Pacific, 1949

CHAPTER 12

A White Woman in South Africa

My fairy Godmother had magicked three mice into horses, a pumpkin into a golden coach and I married a Prince. I am now living in nirvana, leading the life of Riley, frivolous and carefree, doing what I want when I want, with nothing on my mind other than my next hairdo, the choice of pink or red for my finger nails or who to invite to the next braai. It is a life radically different from that I had always known. I am a white woman in South Africa.

I am not a sports type. Poor coordination saw me stuck on top of the wooden horse in the school gym; never put at attack or defense on the netball team. Here in South Africa, three afternoons a week I am serving countless defaults to tennis-mad housewives and at night hitting little balls into holes on a floodlit golf course.

The White Man's Burden

I am a white woman accompanying my husband with my children to complete his temporary contract in Johannesburg, South Africa. My skin is 'white', though in truth – if it is of any importance – it is a pale shade of pink. I was not born in South Africa. I was born in England. I was not schooled in South Africa. I have not worked in South Africa. I have no family lineage in South Africa except that my father's brother, my uncle, immigrated to Cape Town in the 1950s. Having made millions from his clothing factory turned into armaments production in the Second World War I suspect he had an eye to the main chance, the potential to make millions more in the manufacture of overalls, and boiler suits for South African black manual workers. I do not speak South Africa's many tribal languages and, since I am neither Boer nor Afrikaner, I do not speak Afrikaans. I am an English ex-pat with no cultural link to this country. To all intents and purposes, I am an independent observer but, I hasten to add, not an impartial observer. At this point in time, I can emphatically say I am a white woman in South Africa.

The white woman's day-to-day life in South Africa is a hectic, social whirl of friends and neighbors for coffee, Sunday afternoon BBQs, drinks by the pool, classes in macramé, pottery,

Bridge, facials, manicures, lunching out, shopping for *haute couture* to-die-for fashion. As a white woman, staff defer to me as "Madam" or "Ma'am," as if I am Queen of England, to my husband as "Sir." My maid serves early morning coffee in the bedroom and afternoon tea on the patio; she washes, irons, tidies and cleans the house, nannies the baby; some, not mine, cook the evening meal for wages that my children would consider newspaper delivery money. Her meal is on the stove all day, a bubbling concoction emitting a sickly smell that permeates the entire house.

Thursdays were a problem for white South African housewives because Thursday was universal maid's night off. Since white Madams could not, or would not cook, a restaurant booking on a Thursday had to be carefully preplanned weeks ahead. On Tuesday nights, however, it was exactly the opposite. On Tuesday nights, white Madams doggedly stopped at home. Theatres were empty and openly touting for business the best house seats readily available at any theatre. Keeping the Madams at home were the continuing episodes of the 1970s television mini-series 'Rich Man, Poor Man,' a saga of rags to riches, happiness to heartbreak. It was a hard, cruel story with no happy ending, a thoroughly soapy soap opera lapped up by the white women of South Africa. Maybe, succinctly, it offered a foretaste of things to come, a dose of reality that human life did not always end happily, that American dreams did not always come true, that the poor are miserable, that wealth cannot buy happiness, that money changes people often for bad. Television has the power to shape perceptions. 'Rich Man Poor Man' gave these ladies a sneak preview into a glaring world of white suffering should democracy ever come to South Africa, a world beyond *Desperate Housewives*.

The White Man's Burden

In total about face to the primitive, austere and demeaning lives of their house staff, white South African women lived the apex of luxury and glamour in beautiful houses lavishly furnished with clear blue effervescent swimming pools, acreages of well-tended gardens, five-car garages, house boys and live-in maids. To be white in South Africa was a guarantee of privilege, wealth, and a lifestyle that was the envy of Europe and America. Here, servants were not just actors in Downton Abbey or Upstairs Downstairs but real human beings but human beings in dehumanized servility.

There are stories from white South African women who left South Africa for the US or the UK who wondered how as teenagers, they had never questioned their elite life-style of white superiority. Brought up with the Apartheid system, it was the way of life of their parents. In their fantasy world, the plight of the black domestic worker was not of concern. The dire living circumstances of the maid were never spoken about at home. The teenagers enjoyed their privileges and accepted the black man's lot as par for the course. Now, as adults, in another country, they compare the different realities and see the disgrace that it was.

Many were deeply concerned at the racial system and participated in local underground anti-apartheid movements but the Government kept a tight hold and any sign of dissension was to put oneself in danger. One could not blame any white woman for fearing to reveal her feelings on the degrading and inhumane slavery that were the conditions of her domestic staff.

There was the white South African woman grateful for her luck to be born Caucasian and for the luxury afforded to her of having a maid but who had conscience about the living conditions and wages of the maid in her employ. There was the white South African woman to whom the conditions of her maid in the small concrete room off the kitchen with no washroom and meager wages never crossed her mind. She saw the thing in the kitchen as nothing more than a robot acting at her every whim. In either case, whether troubled or not, it had to be true she was aware of the looming threat and consequences there would come if ever there was black majority rule. If there was violence, she would risk having sons at war, she could lose her home, her husband's living, the situation could be untenable and the family would have to flee. Just where the white South Afrikaner would go is debatable. Afrikaans, a derivation of German and Dutch, is not spoken in any other country.

The suffering of those in the hands of the Apartheid regime was a burden that was hard to bear for anyone who was at all thinking and compassionate. I met many South African English who were no longer able to handle the stress and left for the safety of Australia, England or Canada. Many years later, in Canada, I became close friends with a white South African woman, a talented artist and teacher. Her decision to leave South Africa was a distressing story. It was the place of her birth, the country she loved but everything went against her principles of justice and equality for all. At the time, South African authorities only permitted emigrants to take out of the country a maximum of thirty-thousand rand which in relation to the Canadian dollar then would have been about ten thousand dollars. She left for a reduced life-style in Canada with materially nothing. Finding houses in Canada of the same scale she had left was financially beyond her reach; she left her acreaged home in South Africa for a rented townhouse in Canada.

The White Man's Burden

At twenty-nine years of age, Adele Gould left South Africa for Canada. In her blog, Adele, a writer and retired social worker, shares the guilt and regret she feels when she reflects upon her years in South Africa's Apartheid era. Hers was a typical South African household employing two servants whose salaries were shamefully low as was the practice at the time. Adele tells of the colored (mixed race) maid servant, Nancy Sampson, who for twenty-two years took care of her family with love and devotion before she passed away in her fifties.

"My story," she writes in her blog, "revolves around Nancy because I believe that the memories I have of my relationship with her epitomize what later fuelled my hatred of Apartheid.

A picture speaks 1,000 words. Despite the fact that Nancy was like a mother to me, I have only one photograph of her. I am mortified.

"In my family there was never any discussion about the meaning or impact of racial discrimination in South Africa. Apartheid was neither discussed nor questioned. This was your garden-variety white South African family of yesteryear. As a child or teenager I did not possess the insight to remove the 'blinkers' from my eyes. Only when I was in my 20s did I begin to awake from the slumber so ingeniously instilled in my family and me by the Apartheid regime. I try hard not to think how many times during my teenage years, Nancy asked me to stop what I was doing for a moment in order to help her with something. But how could I have helped? I was far too busy luxuriating in the pleasures reserved for white South Africans.

"The South Africa in which I grew up did not teach me to look beyond my own self-serving needs when interacting with non-white people. I would never have dared to refuse to help a white adult! I cringe when I think about the ten-foot-square room in which my beloved Nancy (like millions of other servants) spent so much of her life – a tiny, dark, cluttered room with no bathroom … a room which served as her bedroom, living room, kitchen and dining room … a room located in the back yard of our lovely home (you know, the one with the swimming pool on the half-acre property!) The vivid picture of these appalling living quarters remains indelibly imprinted in my mind's eye, and leaves me feeling heartsore and ashamed. Entertaining spouses in this tiny, hopelessly inadequate room was a recipe for disaster.

"No household was immune to the frequent midnight police invasion of the servants' quarters to catch a spouse spending a night with his wife and to arrest him (often brutally) because he did not carry his pass (I recoil at the very use of that word). Unlike most non-white South Africans who had live-in positions with the Madam, Nancy had a home to which she returned on her days off (which were few, typical at that time). One day I offered to give her a ride, since it was raining. When we were almost there she asked to be dropped off a little distance away. Not wanting to have her walk in the rain, I ignored her request but quickly regretted this when I realized that I had taken away what little dignity she could salvage, for her home was a small, corrugated iron shanty inhabited by who-knows-how-many of her family members. I remember how, in earlier years, Nancy used to tell me she was waiting for a 'council house' – whatever that meant. How would I know? I never stopped to ask! Of course, they never got this council house. *Why, oh why didn't I hear the plea behind that piece of information? Why didn't I listen? Why didn't I try to help?"*

As Adele emerged from oblivion, she saw and felt at the very deepest level the horrors perpetrated in the name of Apartheid laws – from her own self indulgency to the inhumane cruelty with which the black people were treated on a daily basis. Adele is just one of many white South African women who experienced the glaring injustices of Apartheid laws and will be healing forever from inner wounds of sorrow and regret.

Many white women sensitive to the issue of the servant situation were reluctant to talk about it; there was a real fear that somehow the authorities might get to hear and come after them. I found the Afrikaner women living in Pytchley Road were largely indifferent to the black/white situation. One said to me "They have different needs to us."

I found that the majority of Afrikaner women stuck to their own; did not interrelate with English whites. In Afrikaner circles, it was not considered befitting to marry a non-Afrikaner but more and more, this was becoming the exception. I did get to hang out with white Afrikaners in Pytchley Road but I was told it was unusual, language was, of course, a barrier. Pytchley Road was in an Afrikaner neck of the woods. However, most hard-line Afrikaners spoke a modicum of English if not good English. A few would deliberately speak little English.

There was no doubt that the head of the South African household is the man. The husband was the bread-winner and took decisions about money. The women looked after the home while the men took care of the big wide world. I found the women somewhat subservient. White Afrikaner women would always defer to their husbands before taking any decision. It was always the guys who took the lead, kept the social diary, signed the contracts, made the holiday plans, ordered the furniture, thought about the kitchen renovation and quipped the jokes, while the white Afrikaner women would remain on show, genteel, decorous, and elegant.

It would be wrong to put all South African women, Afrikaners or English, under the same umbrella. Times were changing and white women did work in offices and retail or in professions. However, overall, the majority of white South African women remained at home queen of their domains as long as they abided by the principles of Apartheid – and their husbands.

As a social worker in my working life, I have facilitated group experiential exercises designed to increase awareness of people's status, broaden perspectives and attitudes through the simple osmosis of being together, listening, seeing how it is for others. One such exercise was about 'human rights.' I start off with the basic premise: "Some people are born into families which have to walk miles for water. Some people are born into families where they can simply turn on a tap." You might like to try this experiential exercise. It is enlightening, inspiring and educational. You feel the reality of the physical experience of individual group participants as they move back or forward as they respond to given questions. Of course, on paper, the emotional effects will be less glaring.

The White Man's Burden

	Take 1 Step Back	Take 1 Step Forward
If your parents worked weekends and nights to support your family, take 1 step back		
If you were able to show public affection without fear or ridicule, take 1 step forward		
If you were ashamed of your clothes or your house, take 1 step back		
If you were bullied while growing up, for something you could not change, take 1 step back		
If you lived in a supportive family environment, take 1 step forward		
If you were able to travel around your country without fear, take 1 step forward		
If you were able to see a doctor when you wanted, take 1 step forward		
If you had books in the house, take 1 step forward		
If you had physical illness, disability or mental illness, take 1 step back		
If you got loans for your education, take 1 step forward.		
TOTAL	**STEPS BACK**	**STEPS FORWARD**

Comments I heard from participants were:

- "Seeing a bunch of people behind you is not a good feeling."
- We learned about slavery at high school, you feel angry for a few days but you realize this is how it is."
- "Being a white woman, I suppose I can step forward."

The White Man's Burden

- "It is weird to step backward when you know you have worked hard,"
- "No amount of hard work or legislation can make it up to you."
- "As a black Canadian woman, I am not sure where I fit on the spectrum."
- "Looking back to see how much further back you can be, makes you appreciate who you were, where you are now and where you could be."

CHAPTER 13

An Ounce of Gold

Philip bought a Krugerrand, a South African gold coin, one of a limited edition with a certificate to confirm its authenticity. There were two types of Krugerrand, the one used as legal tender made of copper gold alloy, the other, a solid one ounce of gold, the proofed Krugerrand for collectors and investors. Philip bought the proofed Krugerrand. Until 1979, the South African Krugerrand dominated the world gold coin investment market. Then the US introduced the American Golden Eagle and Canada the twenty-four carat Gold Maple Leaf both of which, subversively, were to become expressions of sanctions against South Africa's Apartheid policy.

Our Krugerrand was tightly enclosed in a sealed crystalline case. The 'Krugerrand' is named for Paul Kruger, the Boer farmer, soldier, political leader and early President of the South African Republic, the Rand the currency of South Africa. 'Rand' means

The White Man's Burden

'reef' a chain of rocks and coral. Johannesburg is built on a reef one hundred kilometers long and twenty-three miles wide – a reef loaded with gold.

Our one ounce of gold is now forty-three years old, a mere baby in terms of world money-markets where gold coins have been retrieved from medieval sunken galleons at the bottom of the ocean.

We have not been over lucky with investments and the purchase was made more for souvenir reasons than for value. However, we paid three hundred rand for our ounce of gold and gold now sells for fifteen hundred dollars an ounce so maybe we did better this time. Our Krugerrand sits in a bank deposit box and is bequeathed to Nicholas. Maybe he will retain it for sentimental reasons but this is in the future and not for me to know. I seldom visit our bank deposit box but at times when I do, the Krugerrand in the palm of my hand relives its long journey to its final destination. Behind every ounce of gold is a tale of grim reality.

In 1979 deep down two miles below, there was a working mine in the Gold Reef City of Johannesburg. At the entrance was an exhibit display of the mine of old. As we entered we became pseudo miners given hard-hats and asked to sign an indemnity to absolve the mine owners of responsibility should we sue them for a horrible disease contracted in the mine shaft or injury should the mine collapse. Fairy tales fling gold dust to create magic; mine-workers inhaled gold dust to contract silicosis and tuberculosis. The list of diseases a miner can contract is seriously long. I was put in mind of those iconic American pharmaceutical television commercials which warn of side-effects to the proffered medication, cancer, suicidal thoughts, bleeding from the rectum, heart attacks, even death; yours to pick –the pill or the disease.

A cage took us down to the second stage of the museum, a walk through a dark tunnel shored up by wood beams, wet and dank, hardly high enough for a man to stand upright. Along the route, there were showcases of figurines shoveling, cutting, blasting, bent low, sweating muscled backs, the gleam of the lamps on their hardhats, the only light in the shaft. We saw an ablution area with cold water showers, shelving of concrete where the miners slept. As we left, we went through a store with little sample bottles filled with gold dust, postcards, books and even a beer hall. It seemed to me very contrived, very touristy.

In those days, the reality was miners worked knee-deep in water, had skin ulcers and foot disease. Mine bosses found it cheaper to provide Wellington boots than to drain the mines. Miners active in labor disputes and subversive activities against the Government would stuff messages for each other into their boots. Boots were also a neat way to conceal pillaged gold. Security at the exits required miners to remove and shake out their boots. At diamond mines too, miners were not above shoving a diamond or two into a sock or shoe.

The gold mines offered a wage nowhere equitable to the risk its workers took but it was a wage all the same. For the uneducated, unskilled, unemployed black South African, working in the mine was not a choice but a necessity. It seems to me, no man would go down a mine unless he had to.

The White Man's Burden

Today's miners have air conditioning, full kitchens, social rooms and quality living quarters. It is a far, far better place than had the miners of old. Today there are heavy duty underground carriers, mechanical crushers and lifts, no more the canary bird sent ahead to detect gas leaks, the pit pony hauling ore to the surface. Building standards make for increased safety but hazards are always possible and mines are by no means foolproof. In 2007, three thousand workers were temporarily trapped underground at the Elands Kraal mine, just outside Johannesburg, after a compressed air pipe ruptured due to internal corrosion. The workers were rescued after the blasting smoke had cleared. Mining is still dangerous and is still hard physical labor swinging a shovel full of heavy rock and grit. An intentional pun is to say it needs grit to work in a gold mine. I am old enough to remember the mines of Wales and northern England at a time when coal was the main source of power; when there were explosions from blastings gone wrong, a solemn line of mothers, wives and sisters at the pithead waiting in agony for news. One of the last remnants of goldmines under Apartheid was the sad sight of men in their sixties trundling oxygen trolleys.

To covet my ounce of gold, I must own my personal greed which enabled the misery of those gold miners. In the Apartheid era, where miners made the white man fat, the interest was in money not in souls. If hell is a real place, it was deep down below the earth in those gold mines where the results of continual blasting, the collapse of a roof was just the course of another day.

Though shaking out Wellington boots was for security reasons, it evolved into a traditional dance. Gum Boot Dancing has become known around the world. The miners' boots used to protect and conceal messages or gold became actors playing many parts. By the 1970s, Johannesburg gumboot dancing was a big tourist attraction. Mine-dancing is quite the art, the stamping of feet, slapping of boots, bare-chested tribal warriors wielding spears, shields coming together to the rhythm of the drums. Mining and music an odd partnership, did the miners dance to escape the grimness of their life? It is a rhetorical question to which I have no answer but the performances were regular and the auditorium was packed. I would hazard a cynical guess that the dancers were professionals and had likely never worked in the mines. After the performance, two of the mine dancers in traditional Zulu dress, spears, and shields posed for a now much treasured photograph with Nicholas and Karen–and for tips.

Gold is paired with beauty and power. People die for it; people adore it. Maybe the allure is its glitter, its color, its imperishability or the difficulty of extracting it. More likely, it is its rarity, the toll it takes on the physical human form to bring it to the surface.

Hundreds of years ago, gold symbolized the wealth of a country. In the United States, they lock up their gold in the deep vaults of Fort Knox. I do not even pretend to understand the complexities of the international monetary market but it seems gold is a safe haven should the world run out of money. While gold has not lost value, it has not performed to its expected heights. The Canadian government gradually sold most of its gold reserves. The world Gold Council states Canada is the only G7 country without a stock pile of hundreds of tons of gold.

A fable about how gold brings happiness and unhappiness.

King Midas and the Golden Touch

King Midas was a very wealthy man with a beautiful daughter. He thought gold made happiness and did not understand that he had enough gold. He obsessed with getting gold and spent his days counting his gold coins. A traveler, who was a Greek God in disguise stopped in the rose garden surrounding the King's palace. Walking in the rose garden, the King saw him there and invited him to spend a few days with him in the palace. When it was time for the traveler to leave, he wanted to thank the King for his kindness. He asked the King what wish he would like to make and promised to grant it. King Midas, obsessed as he was with getting more gold to bring him more happiness, wished for everything he touched to be turned to gold. He was warned to think hard about his wish but he was determined and so the traveler granted his wish. King Midas went to bed thinking what a lucky fellow he was to meet such a generous man.

Excitedly, he waited to see if his wish would come true. He touched a small table and it turned to gold. Then he touched a chair, a vase, a clock, the staircase, the doorknob and the flowers on his patio, they all instantly turned to gold. He was overcome with happiness. Overjoyed, he sat down to eat his breakfast. On the table there was a bowl of fruit. He took a grape which turned to gold. The same thing happened with his toast and his bacon and eggs.

He was hungry for breakfast and there was nothing to eat but gold. He began to realize that, in wishing for more gold, he had been cursed. His daughter entered the room, the daughter who was so very beautiful and whom he loved more than anything even more than gold. He touched her long locks and they turned to gold. "What have you done, father?" said the child. In despair, he prayed and asked for forgiveness. The stranger heard his prayer and felt sorry for him. His thoughts became King Midas's thoughts and the King went down to the river to wash away the curse. As he did so, gold came off his fingers flowing into the river. Soon, he was able to touch the river and the water no longer changed to gold. He returned to his house – everything he touched stayed as it was.

King Midas learned his lesson well. He learned that gold, no matter how much you have, does not bring true happiness. He became grateful for the small things in his life, his daughter, his wife, his health, his flowers. He shared his wealth with his people and when he died, they mourned their beloved king.

King Midas finally learned that gold is not synonymous with happiness. In the context of the development of South Africa's gold mining industry, this is, oh, so true. Gold in South Africa brought tragedy not happiness to the black population.

There were nations that refused to buy the Krugerrand because of its association with Apartheid. During the 1970s, it was illegal to import Krugerrands. On our return to the UK in 1979, had English Customs & Excise found the small sealed, proofed Krugerrand in our baggage, I wonder what the penalty would have been. In our own defense, we were ignorant of the embargo on Krugerrands at the time but innocence is never considered an excuse for ignorance.

As for our Krugerrand, it speaks to all that is happy in my life; my wonderful husband my amazing children, our good health, and the opportunity to live in this great country of Canada. However, it has not brought me riches. Maybe, unlike King Midas, I am not obsessed enough!

CHAPTER 14

"We can Change South Africa on the Rugby Field"

– Danie Craven, 1938

Our family had considerable history with the game of rugby football. My mother-in-law had three sons all of whom played rugger. In 1925, my father-in-law founded The Centaurs Rugby Club in England, a club that continues to this day.

To see major sports today is outrageously expensive. An international sports event is outside the pockets of many families, the best alternative an afternoon of chips and beer around the television. When Philip was a boy, ticket prices to first-class sports events were family friendly; the brothers were able to see international matches at Twickenham Rugby Field known affectionally as 'Twickers'. I knew nothing about rugby football or any ball game for that matter. When you marry a rugby guy you get a built-in coach to explain rugger's rules. Up to then all I knew was the public perception of rugby as a sport for hyper-egoed young males, tough and rough, a body-contact game to beat the shit out of the opposing team and come together afterwards for beer and male bonding. In *The Art of Coarse Rugby*, Michael Green defines a Coarse Rugby player "as one that does not enjoy playing but instead plays for any one of a number of other reasons such as to get away from his wife or because he dare not admit he is too old."

When the sun shines all day, outdoor activities come as naturally as sea and sky. South Africans excel at sports whether tennis, cricket, golf, track and field, boxing, soccer or rugby. The international sports world was more concerned with equality of race than sports excellence. South Africa was banned from participating in the 1964 Summer Olympics because it publicly announced the deliberate policy to exclude non-white players from its team. It was banned from the Davis tennis cup in 1971, briefly reinstated in 1973, and banned again in 1978.Cliff Drysdale, South Africa's white Davis Cup tennis player retired from international competition because he was tired of feeling like a pariah. "We played a tie where seventy percent of the spectators were actually protesters." White South Africans felt sports sanctions were far more effective in their impact on the National Party's racial policies than were the world's commercial and industrial sanctions. The famous South African Rugby Springboks were banned from the Rugby World Cups of 1987 and 1991 because of Apartheid boycott.

> *"With regard to abilities, it has been found, among other things that the Japanese cannot jump very high. As far as can be established, no Japanese has yet set a world record in the high jump. This inability is an inherited one because the legs of Japanese are generally too short to shine in this sport.*

The White Man's Burden

Although the Negroid male can generally run fast and has already established many world records in this sport, we do not find hammer throwers or pole vaulters of note among this race. According to experts this inability is due to a shortcoming in coordination with which the Negroid is born. For interest's sake, the reader can try to determine how many full-blooded Negroids, Australoids or even Mongols have ever played in a final in the annual Wimbledon Tennis Championships"

J. D. Versfeld in Saak Vir Afsonerlike Ontwikkeling, 1984

It would take an exceptional person to hit upon the idea of ball sport to knit together a nation. That exceptional person was Nelson Mandela. Soccer balls are cheap to come by and black players took to soccer with a passion. When you kicked around a ball, you forgot the cold, the hunger and the living conditions. Rugby football was an Afrikaner game with a diehard following of Afrikaner fans. Mandela wondered whether the white-dominated sport of rugby could grip the black and colored soccer mad populations. Mandela knew his country. He knew how much respect and pride was given to sport. He knew also many young, white Afrikaners lived in a befuddled world of black and white interrelations and he knew the black community was a forgiving community. Way back in 1938, a decade before Apartheid became official policy, Danie Craven, then a Springboks' scrumhalf, a coach and a Professor of Education, popularly known as Doc or Mr. Rugby, said "We can change South Africa on the Rugby field." Nelson Mandela ran with Danie's idea, a chance and a risk which could have floundered big time.

The White Man's Burden

At the beginning of his Presidency, Mandela sent an invitation to François Pienaar, the then Captain of the Springboks Rugby team, to join him for tea. They talked of everything except sport. In a newspaper interview, François Pienaar said: "I remember when I heard Nelson Mandela's name mentioned at barbecues or dinner parties that the words 'terrorist' or 'bad man' came to mind. As a young kid, I now wish I had questions about it, but I never did. It was not a time when we engaged with our parents and I went along with the thought the guy's not a good guy. You didn't ask questions like why black kids don't go to school with you, why is school just all white? That's how you grew up, which is very wrong and very sad. I wish I'd had the courage to ask questions but I didn't." The Mandela charm over a cup of tea disarmed any assumptions the Rugby team captain had of a 'bad man' or a 'terrorist.'

I would give much to have been at the world Rugby Cup that Saturday, the 24th June, 1995 when South Africa's first multi-racial International team played the New Zealand All Blacks. Ellis Park Stadium, Johannesburg, was packed to capacity, 63,000 people of whom 62,000 were white. The small number of black rugby fans intermingled freely, no longer relegated to a far corner. As Nelson Mandela arrived at the Stadium, he had an idea and he dispatched one of his staff on an errand.

In a thrilling final, South Africa defeated the New Zealand All Blacks 15 to 12, one 'try' in extra time. As the South African players lined up to receive the Cup, a tall black man walked out on to the pitch, the President of South Africa dressed in the green and gold colors of the Springbok rugby team. The black man shook hands with the blond Afrikaner Springbok Captain and between them they held aloft the World Cup. That day something stirred in the hearts of blacks and whites in the Stadium. It was the transformation to mutual racial acceptance, love and brotherhood. I cannot imagine the emotion, the excitement, that day in South Africa when black and white came together for the first time as one nation.

A great leader with a fantastic vision had realized it was not through bloodshed, not through diplomacy or through politics, but through sport that blacks and whites could find mutual respect and trust. White and black spectators cheered together, stood together in a moving rendition of the new National Anthem "Nkosi Sikelel iAfrika" (God Bless Africa). That moment in time has become an iconic moment in South Africa's history.

White South African Gary Player, one of the world's foremost golf players, won the US Open three times. In his early years, Gary Player was a known supporter of Prime Minister Verwoerd and his system of Apartheid. Later in life, he recalled how easy it is to influence the young for good or bad. The young Gary Player was simply brainwashed by the system of the time. Since then, he has spent much of his life traveling the world's golf courses, seeing other ways of living, and his vision of his native country changed. So shameful did he feel, he publicly announced his changed beliefs. For his alleged racism, Gary Player suffered many indignities. In 1969 at the US PGA Championship, a group of militant demonstrators who opposed apartheid yelled in the middle of his swing in an attempt to disrupt his play. At one point, ice was thrown at him and spectators tried to rush him. In Australia, in the middle of the night, protestors etched on the green, 'Go home, you racist pig' in white lime. Many South African athletes recognizing they had little chance of sports success in South Africa, left for other countries. Nelson Mandela praised Gary Player for being an ambassador of truth for South Africa, steadfast to his principles. The Gary Player Foundation furthers education among young black people; Nelson Mandela served as a trustee.

Arthur Ashe the American born black tennis champion was a hero to black South Africans. For years, the Apartheid government vetoed his Visa to South Africa. He finally did come to play in South Africa's National Tennis Tournament in November 1973. He wanted South Africa to see a black man playing tennis against a white man. In the South African Open, Arthur Ashe beat top international white tennis stars Cliff Drysdale and Bob Hewitt; he was the first black man to break the sports color barrier in South Africa. That day, white Afrikaner morale took a beating physically and mentally. Arthur Ashe still remains today the only black man to win a Wimbledon singles title.

Sport has been called a civic religion in South Africa, but if it was, then that civic religion was instrumental in beginning the two-decade process of dismantling Apartheid.

CHAPTER 15

The Story of Kamau

Kamau is fourteen. Kamau is black. His mother, Chikondi is also the mother of his three sisters. He did not know his father or who fathered his sisters. "Kaffirs breed like rabbits," he heard a white man say. Kamau grew up in Alexandra Township, twelve kilometers northeast of Johannesburg. Alexandra was a town of one million in a mile of squalor, polluted streets, overcrowded shacks, fifty percent unemployment and desperate poverty. Alexandra had no electricity. Drinking water came from communal taps, one tap serving several households. Rats were everywhere in the town, scrawny cats becoming fat cats.

It was not in the interests of the Apartheid Government to have an educated black population. Educated black people might run for public office, start a coup to take the Government down. Worse, they would not want to work in the mines or be domestic workers. Bantu education was intended to dampen those who aspired to ambition through academic learning. Bantu education was restricted to practical learning; ample for people who worked only in the mines, factories or domestic service. The syllabus was reading, writing and arithmetic, poems by rote, African tribal singing, cooking, sewing, carpentry. Kamau could just about read a few simple sentences, count to one hundred and sign his name.

Most pupils dropped out of school before the end of primary education. There were a few black elite who somehow got to go on to secondary education, maybe matriculated, worked in offices, owned a betting shop, a shebeen or food store. Through ardent persistence and determination, a very few might get a bursary, make it into law, accounting, medicine. When they graduated, these ambitious and bright black men could serve only the black community.

An honest job would have fueled the self-worth of men aimlessly languishing round the streets of Alexandra, returning to the shack only to beat the wife – and often there was more than one wife. Infidelity was the norm. When there was not enough money for food or rent, there was the shebeen to douse away the bad spirits. The shebeen was a local hole, a meeting place for black men to gamble and drink and where working class activists gathered. It served unlicensed brews and was totally illegal. If you lucked out gambling, you could use the proceeds to drink yourself into a stupor, become oblivious to this hell on earth, go home to beat the wife again. Black children knew violence well. It was the way of life.

Children who failed a test, talked in class, passed secret notes, dropped a pencil or took a day off for a cold, well knew the sjambok, a long stiff whip of rhinoceros hide propped up against the teacher's desk. Kamau often came to school without breakfast. Concentrating was difficult on an empty tummy and he often failed tests. Kamau knew the sjambok. It was tough to survive school. He had supposed teachers were there to help him learn. What manner of teacher whipped a pupil for failing a test?

In 1979, there was little in the township to hold the interest of a teenager's ever-enquiring mind. Alexandra had no ball park, boys club, cricket pitch, public library or swimming pool. In Johannesburg, the three public swimming pools were *'Slegs Blankes'* – 'Whites Only'. Scores of black kids played homespun soccer using makeshift dump yards to kick around a ball.

Every black man or woman over sixteen had to carry a dompas, a passbook, which contained name, tribe, age, birthplace, employment status and history; employers often entered a behavioral evaluation of work conduct in the dompas. It was illegal for any black African to be in a white area without a passbook even if he had been born or lived in a neighboring township.

Alexandra was one such township, a major source of black labor for Johannesburg and its suburbs. The police did random checks; a black South African without a pass would be immediately arrested, arraigned in court where he stood to be deported to his Homeland. To find work, many black Africans who had no pass violated the laws. It was implicit to keep a wary eye open for policemen, particularly black policemen. For a bribe, black policemen would overlook an invalid or missing passbook.

Kamau had attended school for four years to Standard 4. His mother could not read but for her son, she wanted better. She was very firm he should learn to read. From her low wages, she scratched out enough to pay for school tuition, books and uniforms. Kamau had not attended school yesterday because of a tummy bug. Today, when the sjambok came down, he withdrew his hand and the sjambok became wildly airborne, was caught by a pupil in the back row to much hilarity. The teacher was outraged and embarrassed. Kamau was expelled. There was always the next boy waiting to be whacked; the line-up of kids to take his place in Standard 4 was long; disobedience, inattention, learning difficulties, all good excuses to advance the line-up.

His opportunity for schooling was gone. But it was okay, he was free to ride his bike when and where. He had a roof over his head, even if it was a corrugated iron roof and a cardboard box on which to lay for sleep. Kamau knew no other way of life. He accepted all because he knew no different.

Bikes were common in Alexandra. Kamau had no money for bus tickets. In any case, he liked to ride the open road; to feel the wind flow through his hair, the skill of negotiating the bumpy, ridged, undulating dirt track where a tire in a rut would put the bike in a spin and throw you off. Kamau loved being away from the stench of garbage, litter and debris strewn around the Alexandra streets, the pull of his muscles straining to climb the hills. He would bike into Johannesburg suburbs, Randburg, Sandton, and Bryanston, through avenues of green trees, past the brick-walled entrance gates of houses set back from the road. As he biked, he wondered about the white men who lived behind those walls. He had met very few white men in his fourteen years. He knew little of how they lived but he knew his mother feared them. Behind the trees and the walls, he could see roofs with tiles, small, patterned windowpanes not roofs of corrugated iron as in Alexandra. Styles and architecture were of no interest to Kamau. He knew shanty hut-like housing, windows with no glass. His interest was the need for a second pair of pants or socks, a blanket for a cold night.

In riding along the quiet avenues outside of Alexandra, Kamau came to know there was a different way to live. He noticed the neatness and orderliness of the roads, the well-kept grassed sidewalks, clipped trees, and the pothole-free pavements. He contrasted this symmetry and quiet calm to the disheveled, unkempt township that was his place of birth. He could see smoke rising from chimneys and supposed the people in these houses were not cold at night as he was. At fourteen, a boy is moving towards awareness of what might be, of things to come and Kamau came to understand that the difference between black and white was not purely the color of skin.

As an uneducated black, his future was in the mine or as a house or garden boy, a golf caddy, a dishwasher, and that was if he was lucky to beat the lineup. It was not an exciting prospect for an intelligent youth embarking on life's adventures. His mother did laundry for white Madams in Randburg and washed dishes at an Alexandra greasy spoon. She worked as many hours as she could and was rarely around to show the love she felt in her heart for her children. Kamau's sisters scavenged for food – wilted, discolored vegetables, meat bones, stale rolls, coal to cook their findings into slap pap or meat bone bredie. His mother returned home late in the evening. She had dark rings round her eyes. She looked older than her forty years. Kamau was a latchkey kid, which was a misnomer because it was unnecessary to lock the shack that was his home. His mother struggled to do what she could for her children. She received no financial support from any of the fathers.

The White Man's Burden

With no parent to instill solid values, a dearth of love, no pride of possession, no goals of achievement or accomplishment, no access to books to widen a limited world, how does a boy grow up to be a man? How does he know his own self-worth, be able to offer kindness to others, be motivated to learn, to achieve, to take his place in society when the white man says, "Blacks are not ready to live like the white man; the vast majority of blacks are still ignorant and uncivilized." The teenage response to the white man was the Tsotsi gang. The roving Tsotsi thugs offered excitement, adventure and, as Kamau believed, friendship.

Kamau and the Tsotsi gang rode beyond Alexandra in a show of ego and aggression designed to prove they were guys to fear although it was fear itself they felt. Gangs of bored, goalless, aimless and hopeless youths in their formative years with unachievable dreams terrorized the town and the white suburbs seeking excitement where there was none. Idle minds became the playgrounds of the devil. Tsotsi gangs, just boys, boys who had taken a wrong turning, a 'black problem' hardened into tough, anti-social, emotionless petty criminals. It was the answer to the Afrikaners' disdain for the color of black skin.

Kamau, a kid from the ghetto, hung round the malls, the smoke stores and beer houses with other Tsotsi teenagers. No one cared what he did or what he did not do. On a Saturday morning, a young white man was unable to find his car parked behind Sandton Mall. Employees at the mall believe it was a Tsotsi gang from Alexandra. A resident stated that, to all intents and purposes, it looked to be a harmless group of teenagers, but she had a sense they were up to no good. A mall employee described how a lady was robbed of her purse right in front of her, and how she barely escaped robbery herself. Kamau watched as the gang stood waiting for their next victim. He had not participated and was uneasy, unsure; friendship was why he hung out, but he had a strong stirring of conscience.

In the many bike rides with the Tsotsi gang, Kamau grew up sharply, from the innocent fourteen-year-old boy he was, to acquire the street smarts of those misled youths on a vendetta to extract return in whatever way they could from the white man who saw them as less than dust.

One of the bike trips took the gang to upscale Bryanston in the Northern suburbs, the wealthy community where a security wall surrounds every house and every gate promises armed response. Out to get their dues from the white man, the gang scoured the roads in this quiet, respectable neighborhood. They were pure trouble. A police car, likely alerted by a householder, drew up alongside the bikers and a black policeman asked them to produce their passbooks. None of them had passbooks. Kamau had no passbook. He was not yet sixteen, the age when he must have a passbook. Unable to produce a passbook when the police asked for it and in an unauthorized area, the Bantu Police arrested them all and took them to jail and from jail to Court in Pretoria for trial. His mother had no passbook, which is why she could not earn better money in Johannesburg. Kamau was illegally living in Alexandra. In truth, there were so many trials going on for black people without passbooks or forgotten passbooks that the courts were backed-up and most times the charges never came before the Magistrate. Released from court, Kamau rode back to Alexandra, forty miles, a long ride.

The White Man's Burden

On an evening bike ride with Gio and Danie to Kensington B, Gio and Danie would knock on doors. If someone answered, they would rush in grabbing what they could and rush out. The evenings were best because when the white man was at home, the entrance gates were more likely to be unlocked and the security alarm off. Gio and Danie unlatched the iron gate to a garden and traversed the crazy-paving to the front door. Kamau held back, following cautiously, fearfully, feeling it was wrong, but afraid of being ridiculed for lack of courage. The two were in and out of the house in a flash. Kamau was too slow to get out and found the front door closed, a white man barring his way.

"Hey, there young man, that's enough," said the man with a bald head and grayish beard. Kamau froze.
"What you got to say for yourself?" Kamau looked down and shuffled his feet. "I didn't take anything, Sir."
"What would your father say if I entered your home uninvited?"
"I don't know, Sir. I don't got no father"
"Why are you with these hoodlums?"
"They are my friends"
"What kinds of friends make a habit of crashing houses, taking peoples' things?"
"Don't know, Sir."
"Where do you come from?"
"Alexandra, Sir."
"Do you go to school?"
"No, Sir. Ain't got no room for me."
"Do you have any family?"
"My mother, Sir, she works at Joe's in Alexandra."
"Does she know what you are doing today?"

The White Man's Burden

"No Sir, she would be very angry."
"Well, I am angry, what do you say to that?"
"You are right to be angry, Sir, I am sorry."
"If you don't go to school, what do you want to do?"
"I want to get a job. I like animals."
"What would you say if I could help you find a job with animals?"
"That would be very good of you, Sir. It would make my mother very happy and we would be able to buy food and clothes."
"Well, come and see me tomorrow at this time and I will let you know if I have been able to do anything for you."
"Sir, you are so kind. I promise not to steal again."
"What's your name?"
"Kamau, Sir."
"Well, Kamau, I think you are a good boy. Don't let me down."
"Sir, I promise I will not let you down. I thank you for not calling the police."
"Everybody deserves a second chance," said the man sententiously.

Kamau left the house, his heart singing. There was kindness among white men. He rode his bike back to Alexandra.

"What happened to you?" said Danie.
"I believe the white man has kindness. He is going to find me a job."
"Ag" said Danie, "never trust a white man, they say anything."
"I trust him," said Kamau.

CHAPTER 16

"You must be on Top of Change or Change will be on Top of You."

– Mark Victor Hansen

The Minister of Defense, General Magnus Malan, speaking at a Rotary Function:

> *"There is no conflict in South Africa between white and black. There is confrontation between civilization and barbarism".*

Cape Times, June 26, 1987

Monopoly, the board game of takeovers, house and hotel buying, wheeling and dealing has never lost its popularity. Indeed, Monopoly has evolved over time, the Star Wars edition, the Digital edition, the World edition and Junior Monopoly setting the kids early on the business trail. Monopoly players in 2017 start with

$15,000 in hand not $1,500, collect $2,000 for passing 'Go' not $200 and pay 10% of total earnings to income taxes. Modern Monopoly takes into consideration cost of living and realistic property prices.

In its original form, Monopoly is simply a game that mimics life in an eerie way. It is the stuff of grinding your opponents to the dust, an introduction and education into ambition and power. Power reflects the human desire for gain and possession, and power was the building block of Apartheid; to have it all at the expense of the vulnerable. History is full of examples of monopoly, the Romans, the Crusaders, the American slave traders, the Rwandan Massacre, the Holocaust, the rise of ISIL and Boko Haram. To conquer or to lose – to draw your bow and arrow, to mount your horse, drive your tanks, fly your unmanned missiles or launch your robot spy planes, it is all monopoly.

By nature I am a 'what if' person. A 'what if' person juggles with the ups and the antes, reverses the consequences and as in a detective story, anticipates the red herrings. Some say because 'what ifs' are unknown factors not reality, they are not worth wasting time on; that dwelling on 'what if's' can be disturbing, 'What if I had answered the phone that night…?" Notwithstanding the rights and wrongs of 'what if's', it is fun to conjure with different outcomes and consequences. What if the Boers in the eighteen hundreds had encountered a refined, cultured, white indigenous people on their trek to the North East Cape, people who lived in brick-built houses with gabled roofs, indoor plumbing, who hunted with guns, farmed with harvesters, cultivated potatoes, went to church? What if there had been no half-naked blacks in primitive round huts, using strange languages and spears and shields, an ungodly lot? Would there have been a civilized round table discussion to negotiate a land agreement rather than the Battle of Blood River in which African Chief, Dingane, lost 3000 Zulu warriors while only three Boers were wounded? There was clearly enough land for both. What if?

The massive black population was a hindrance to the Afrikaner plan. If you cannot slaughter them in mass genocide, then Plan B is to suppress and subordinate them. The big plan of separation was Grand Apartheid. The big plan was to be seen as charitable. The Afrikaners would be magnanimous, giving away portions of their hard-fought-for lands to each tribe and declaring each chunk an independent, self-governing state. Now what nation would do that? The blacks would live in the 'Homelands', which would leave South Africa, all white. Wunderbar! The Master Plan would be accomplished except that the Homelands which the Afrikaners gave to the black tribes were barren, infertile without industry or commerce and with limited access to the ocean. In his gift to black South Africa, the white Afrikaner had overlooked the fundamentals of humanity, the provision of shelter, food, education and employment. It is hardly rocket science to reason that the white Afrikaner knew that uneducated, unskilled humans, black or white, would be unable to transform the Homelands into life-sustaining communities. The black workers would have no choice but to do what was intended for them all along, to seek work in South Africa. The Homelands project was nothing more than a dumping ground to rid South Africa of its blacks; to have one's cake and eat it as it were, to leave the working black population far away but sufficiently near to the mines or domestic sector. It is cause to reflect were the settlers who half a century earlier displaced Canada's indigenous peoples any different? Was the reservation system imposed on Canada's indigenous peoples any different to the Homelands imposed on South Africa's tribal peoples?

Some years ago there was a television commercial depicting the "Kodak baby," the sweet, innocent face of a newborn coming in this world with a completely blank slate, asking for nothing more than love and nurture. Newborns bring with them a sensory world of sound, touch, smell, and sight. The infant grows in a mix of family life, the social world and inherited genes. The Brady Bunch, the perfect family, had scripted family values but there is no script for real life and no perfect family. We all have to do our best and hope we have given our kids a solid foundation of family values to cope with whatever life throws at them.

> If a child lives with criticism,
> She learns to condemn.
> If a child lives with hostility,
> He learns to fight.
> If a child lives with ridicule,
> She learns to be shy.
> If a child lives with shame,
> He learns to feel guilty.
> If a child lives with tolerance,
> She learns to be patient.
> If a child lives with encouragement,
> He learns confidence.
> If a child lives with praise,
> She learns to appreciate.
> If a child lives with fairness,
> He learns justice.
> If a child lives with security,

The White Man's Burden

> She learns to have faith.
> If a child lives with approval,
> He learns to like himself.
> If a child lives with acceptance and friendship,
> She learns to find love in the world
>
> *Anonymous*

Feigning the innocence of an ex-pat from England, I asked a white Afrikaner why he thought Afrikaners reviled the black man in South Africa. Could he humor me to explain his attitude and that of his people? "Our problems are unique," he answered me. "You've got to be a white Afrikaner South African to understand. The black man in our country is a colossal burden and we carry that burden more successfully than any other African country. Look, we are three million Whites caring for twenty-two million Blacks. We sacrificed ourselves to come to this land, trekking long and far, pioneering the unknown to find a place to call home. We did not live in mud huts and carry spears; we built houses, seeded our farms and milked our cattle. We financed the gold and diamond industry, the oil industry. We brought prosperity, wealth, industry and business to South Africa and we made South Africa among the richest nations in the world. This is our country. It is our God-given right to be here. Afrikaans is our language, not spoken in any other country. We did the right thing. We made a plan to help the black population become citizens in their own home-lands; free to govern themselves independently; free to exercise their culture in their tribal lands. Isn't that the idea of democracy, free citizens in their own lands with all the rights of government and independence? We are not the Israelis who allow millions of Arabs to dwell in nowhere land. Of our own free will we have given our precious land to the black population for their own use to thrive and prosper. I ask you, where would the black man be without us?"

> *"Reduced to its simplest, the problem is nothing else than this: we want to keep South Africa white. Keeping it white can only mean one thing, namely, white domination"*

(quoted from the UNESCO Courier, April 1965).

We want to keep South Africa white, that is how a white Afrikaner saw it. The world saw it differently. The world saw blatant racism, a collective psychopath without compassion or feeling that trashed the very core of its indigenous populace and peoples of color. Musing, I wondered if there is such a thing as a collective psychopath and, if so, would the characteristics of the white Afrikaners classify for membership. A psychopath is after all charming, intelligent, a 'lekker' fellow, the right guy to have as a next door neighbor except that beneath that nice exterior lurks callousness, a lack of empathy, a blurring of right from wrong. Psychologists would say there is no collective psychopath but they do not deny there is the individual psychopath. Psychopathic leaders charm us all, their skills are in being personable, impressive, driven – Stalin, Mao, Lenin, Hitler and Kim Jong-un. I am not for rubber-stamping people into groups, genres or pigeonholing society because I have huge faith in the individual goodness of human kind. That said, cultural stereotyping does take place; we hear it all the time. The Scots are stereotyped as frugal, the Americans egotistical, the French good lovers, the Canadians polite, the Welsh musical and the Afrikaner efficient, organized, self-disciplined, the quintessential policeman, farmer and, apparently, good dentists.

The White Man's Burden

There were white South African writers, activists, clergymen and journalists who put themselves out there front and centre to align with the struggle to bring down the National Government. One such activist was white South African, Helen Suzman, of the Progressive Federal Party the official opposition to the National Government. At the time, Helen Suzman was the Party's only sitting MP and the only female Member of Parliament. She was often harassed by the police and her phone tapped. She had a special technique for dealing with eavesdropping, which was to blow a whistle into the mouthpiece of the phone. It would be thirteen years before her opposition party was joined by other party colleagues.

Father Trevor Huddleston from England, whose pulpit was in a black township in the 1950s, was a thorn in the side of the Apartheid regime and renowned for his outspokenness and activism. No one did more to keep Apartheid on the world agenda than Trevor Huddleston. In his book 'Naught for Your Comfort', Trevor Huddleston wonders which side Jesus would have sat in a room where blacks sat on one side and whites sat on the other. Which side to sit with; how to be on both sides, neatly sums up the dilemma for the white Christian committed to the ideals of his faith.

It seemed to me that committed Christians would have mixed feelings about a church that talked the talk but did not walk the walk – love thy neighbor, heal the poor, the meek shall inherit the earth, do unto others what you would have them do unto you." Sunday church for most white Afrikaners had to be a conflict between self-concern and conscience. To attend church and to know less than ten miles away was a shanty town with no heat, no water, people starving, had to be hypocrisy. The principles and ideals of the faith were not the focus of Sunday church; tradition, culture and social life were. I met many Madams who attended Sunday morning church but did not give their maid Sunday morning off. That being said, it could not have been easy for Christians true to their principles, Afrikaans or English. Even the smallest activism against the status quo had the very real possibility of being branded anti-Apartheid, communist, terrorist punishable by imprisonment, torture or death.

There were also thousands of black freedom fighters fighting for justice and many working clandestinely underground. One such freedom fighter was, O.R. Tambo who, when detained under house arrest by the South African Government for activism, went underground and later joined the vibrant and growing anti-Apartheid movement working against the regime in London.

Many English South Africans say it was very difficult to live with their conscience and with the total inability to make change. There was a sense that white English South Africans lived in a bubble, were not engaged in the lived experience of South Africa and were in denial of what was happening around them. It was a time of complexity and fear and people who could not be true to themselves.

To sum up, there were the English South Africans who went with the flow, more concerned with business, the big house, braais, tennis and macramé, there were the English South Africans opposed to the racist regime but rendered totally powerless to do anything about it; there were the few English South Africans in active opposition and there was the white Afrikaner, hard-wired in his stance for an all-white South Africa. It should be said there were a few enlightened white Afrikaners who saw the writing on the wall and inevitable change. "I'm a recovering racist," said a white Afrikaner South African, "I have a lot to do in terms of healing."

The National Government and the South African Defense Force were strong and controlling. Given my druthers, I would have liked to let loose my rage in some show of protest against racism, a march perhaps. I was an outsider – if I were chucked out what did it really matter? To be honest, I did not have the courage. Also, it was hard not to get sucked into the life-style of the rich and not so famous, a poor excuse but the reality of the vast majority of white South Africans who stood by and said nothing, waiting for Godot, as it were. When you are one of three million among twenty-two million, fear overtakes good intentions.

A progressive journalist who did not fare well was Donald Woods, editor of the East London Daily Dispatch in South Africa's Cape Province who described himself as a white liberal. He spent years publicly opposing racial segregation until he was finally placed under house arrest, his telephone bugged, banned for five years from working, travelling, writing or speaking publicly. His six-year-old daughter was severely burned after putting on a T-shirt she received in the mail which had been soaked in acid. Fearing for his life, he escaped by jumping a high fence disguised as a priest, hitchhiked three hundred miles and swam the Tele River in the Eastern Cape from where he fled to England. "I could no longer function here as a journalist" he said

The English South African Press opposed Apartheid in a veiled way, by innuendo and satire. It was a difficult job for an honest, objective, speak-your-mind journalist but those who

The White Man's Burden

did speak out mainly got away with it. Providing balanced media was a struggle. Small items would seep through comparing South Africa's very rich and very poor; its high standard of living and its absence of social services for marginalized residents. Uprisings and demonstrations were mostly reported in the guise of criminal offences not in the political sense.

Many opposition perspectives were delivered through satire. In the Johannesburg Star, the "Day by Day" cartoons of Abe Berry highlighting the everyday lives of Maids and Madams were a regular feature. To add context to explain the cartoon below, the political and economic affairs of the black population in the Transvaal were administered by the West Rand Administrative Board.

Music comes naturally to black South Africans, a music genre uniquely their own, in indigenous languages of song, chant and rhythm inspiring strength and hope to overcoming hardship. Hundreds of bands emerged from the Homelands often acapella, mostly guitar and drums. Big names to come were Village Pope and Black Jesus. Towards the end of Apartheid, rebellious rock, funk and rap blatantly conveyed direct messages to the National Government for freedom. "Toyi-Toyi" is an Apartheid resistance chant. The crowd chanted "Toyi-Toyi", the leader called out, "Amandla!" ("Power") and the group response was "Awethu!" ("Ours").As one activist puts it, "Toyi-toyi" was our weapon. We did not have tear gas and tanks, but we had music". The United Nations issued a proclamation to musicians to boycott South Africa. 'Artists United' was a political message from outside South Africa, a protest group which included Bob Geldof, Bob Dylan, Bonnie Raitt, Bruce Springsteen, Darlene Love, Miles David, Ringo Starr, Pete Townsend, Peter Gabriel, Steve Van Zandt and many others.

Western music trickled into South Africa through tapes and records but mainly black South Africans were short ordered on pop music of the era. The South African Broadcasting Corporation banned Beatles records because of John Lennon's Hallelujah and his radio statement: "I don't know which will go first, rock 'n' roll or Christianity" as well as the recordings of many other major musicians.

As was my custom, morning coffee got me tuning into Springbok Radio, a commercial Johannesburg affiliate of SABC, designed to appeal to the white English-speaking and suburban stay-at-home housewife. In context of the serious black situation, Springbok Radio was shallow and trivial. I felt tears of loathing when I listened to the droll, trite offerings of Springbok Radio talk shows advising me to 'put my face on before my husband awoke' and 'a lace table cloth on an ironing board would make a good substitute for a coffee table.' All this nonsense while seven miles away, people were starving, scratching for food scraps from garbage bins, cold and debased.

The White Man's Burden

The great classical composers were virtually unknown to the black South African. Yehudi Menuhin, the virtuoso violinist, while in Johannesburg, asked to perform for a black audience. He was told he would be breaking his contract. In defiance, he threatened to pressure world-renowned artists not to visit South Africa. His zealousness worked as he did get to play in the small church hall of the black shanty town, Sophia town.

Few of us follow through on our convictions, actually put words into action, "walk- the-walk" as it were. From time to time, there are heroes and heroines so staunch in their convictions they just have to help. In 1970s South Africa, a quiet, unassuming couple, Ad and Wal were two such people. Theirs is the story of an ordinary couple who did extraordinary things despite the odds, two modest people who did what they thought was right and became notorious for it. Her full name was Adelaine Hain, but she went under "Ad." She was the conventional homemaker though this was South Africa when a maid to do the washing and cleaning went with the territory. However, it was Ad who did the cooking and Ad who took care of the kids. Wal was an Architect. Routinely, Wal went to work and returned home to the wife and kids. That this ordinary couple became enemies of South Africa, briefly imprisoned, constantly harassed by security services and ultimately forced into exile is the stuff of fiction except it is true. Born and raised in South Africa during the era of British Colonialism, the Hains knew full-well the system of racism and class. Ad's family was strongly religious; their church was okay with different races and from an early age, Ad was used to treating black people as equals, with not much of a thought to its political implications. When she saw faith used to justify prejudice, she came to question herself. She could see no Christianity in the way black people were treated.

The White Man's Burden

It was not the way of Jesus, "the meek shall inherit the earth", "love one another as I have loved you." Ad saw black people as decent folk with good family traditions, love of their culture, no different, just people like her. She came to witness another system more drastic than British Colonialism. Rules were coming from Parliament about where black people could live, where they could work, where they could go. A new word was coined – Apartheid, meaning her maid had to be documented, to carry a pass, jailed if found without it, no access to theatres, swimming pools, park seats marked "whites only" as were toilets. She knew of the black slums of Sophiatown and other shantytowns where there was no electricity, no clean drinking water and only outdoor toilets. Ad, fervently passionate, volunteered to help black offenders and their families receive bail and free legal help, visited black families to supply food and clothing. In her mission, she found there was a community of black and white South Africans opposed, like her, to the cruelty of Apartheid. One of these was Dikgang Moseneke (who is now Deputy Chief Justice in South Africa's Supreme Court). "Ad did much to form my own notions of a non-racial South Africa because she cut across lines that were thought eternal."

Ad's voluntary work and insurgency came to the attention of the South African Government. She had committed no crime but she was banned from continuing her activities and ordered to attend weekly meetings with the police. Ad and Wal's phone was tapped, mail intercepted and police patrolled the house. Special branch officers pillaged the children's' toys and scrapbooks vainly seeking information. Ad and Wal were not terrorists or spies, they were just concerned people who saw a wrong and wanted to right it. Advocacy was their nature, violence was not. They wanted no truck with violence; their interventions were peaceful. However, in the

1970s, violence came to them when a bomb exploded in the whites-only courtyard of Johannesburg's railway station. Twenty-four people were badly hurt and one died. Weeks after the bombing, it was discovered that the person responsible for the bombing was John Harris. John was a friend of Ad and Wal and the family was shattered by the news. The John Harris they knew was a stable, liberal-minded, white South African. John Harris was put on trial for treason and sentenced to death. The effect of the bombing was to heighten government and police controls on the lives of everyday folk. On the Hain family, police surveillance increased. Wal lost his job, and his notoriety left him unemployable. The Government took no chances and exiled the Hains from South Africa. The epicenter for the world Anti-Apartheid movement was London, England. In London, England, Ad and Wal found they could fulfill their mission in a very different way even from eight thousand miles away.

Ad and Wal's advocacy came from their own deep commitment to create right out of wrong. Their strength was their strong commitment to each in a long marriage. Ad and Wal lived to see the end of Apartheid, the start of majority rule, and they returned to South Africa. Al and Wal's son, Peter, was shocked to find his parents involved with a revolutionary. Peter Hain became a British MP, Cabinet Minister and, in 2015, a Life Peer.

South Africa's racial discrimination cost it the respect of the world and the leadership of the African continent. Yet Africa remained an ostrich, its head in the sand, the messenger of its own demise. It was expected the Afrikaner government would not loosen its hold without civil war, the Afrikaners smug in their belief South Africa was God-given to them as an all-white nation.

The White Man's Burden

At the end of our two years in South Africa, I left convinced that Apartheid was not for the long haul. I had seen the Afrikaner Government noticeably soften. Younger Afrikaners, unlike generations before them, discovered a new word, 'multiculturism,' ethnic identities living together in peace and harmony and knew something was wrong in their part of the world. Government began to heed public calls for concessions to 'petty Apartheid', permitting mixed races on buses, in public swimming pools and theatres. Nevertheless, hardline Apartheid was still strong particularly in inter-racial marriage, sports, the black vote and the dompas but there were those in the Afrikaner Government quietly listening.

I am not sure whether it is possible ever to eradicate total racial discrimination. Prejudice lurks insidiously quietly hidden within us all. Gay prejudice comes from the same stable, just a horse of a different color. As I write, it is Gay Pride week in Canada with thousands participating in roadside celebrations to be sexually different, pride for their uniqueness, crowds lining the streets in support of that freedom. Rainbow flags, balloons and streamers fly high above extravagant floats, elaborate and outrageous costumes of neon and spandex, conveying messages of hope for acceptance of all differences. From London UK, a South African was quoted as saying, "We don't have anything like this in South Africa. It's so exciting and creative and it takes a lot of guts for them to do this. South Africa is still very conservative. I think something like this opens people's minds."

South Africa is undergoing Truth and Reconciliation processes. I recently watched a video of ex-President F.W. De Clerk's apology for the National Government's policy of separateness. He said Apartheid as a system was not meant to be harmful to society but to provide a structured democratic setup for the eleven tribes of indigenous people. Asked directly to apologize for the inhumanity of it, he spluttered and mumbled finding it difficult to let the words escape his lips, which they never did. The last White President of South Africa did concede to black democracy but he had to bite his tongue to do so.

> When you see someone who needs power and control and will not stop until they get it, you are actually seeing someone who is deeply afraid of life.
> Fearful people can only have things their way.

CHAPTER 17

Power Point Presentation
'Post–Apartheidarity'

As heard on the streets

- Ten years ago, black people could not mix with whites; black people could not shop at the same shop as white people. Now black and white work in offices, shops, government and blacks can marry white people.

- At work on the farm, I am well treated and given respect. The farm has changed for the better in the past ten years, but the African National Congress is not delivering. There is no running water or electricity on the farm.

- I have applied to own the farm and to get an agriculture subsidy. In the past, only whites would work as managers. We blacks could not own land.

- In the new South Africa, they have to talk to you properly.

- The change is whether black culture takes over or if blacks become westernized.

- You can see the difference in how the streets look – it is very different.

- I am a Grade 1 teacher in Alexandra Township. I am happy with the curriculum changes, but overcrowding is a big issue. I have 50 students in my class but at least we have equipment like TVs and books now and computers, everything technological.

- High schools have big problems with high dropout rates but the Rainbow Nation will slowly get there.

- We can go to places we have never been, theatres, movies, restaurants. Back then, I could only sit on a 'blacks only' park bench.

- There has been a little change, not a lot.

- The housing scheme is bad – they build houses into which you cannot fit your bedroom suite.

- We are not the generation that will really enjoy the new freedoms but are preparing the ground for our children and future generations.

The White Man's Burden

- I am soon to go on a tourism course paid for by the government and am hopeful about the future.

- My country's place in history is not doubted but the perception is still of black townships, shacks, poverty, violence, a no-go area for those with a white face.

- Tourists see historical landmarks, homes of some of South Africa's most famous people – Nelson Mandela, Desmond Tutu – they see everything from shacks to mansions.

- Soweto is a place of contrasts – a boy in the township became a top-flight businessman in the new South Africa.

- Soweto is not a place of doom and gloom; it is a place of hope where people come for inspiration.

- Soweto's children have grown up with democracy. Sowetans have a real passion and optimism for their township. Just visit one of the thousands of shebeens – the bars and clubs scattered across the city – you will feel it.

- The vibe has always been here but today it is not hidden. It is shouted from the rooftops.

- For years, the energy and the heart of South Africa have been trapped in the townships, but now they have been released to the country at large.

- The biggest problem for me here in Soweto is lack of jobs. I have not worked in a proper job for ten years.

- I come from a half-apartheid, half-democracy. These kids are inheriting the 100% pure fruits of democracy. These kids are the future and these kids will take the message to the world.

- If you want to see poverty, you can see poverty, but it is vibrant, it is colorful and it's a place which helped to change the political life of South Africa.

- I am a contractor working at platinum mine on machines and riding underground trains. It is 2 km down and takes half an hour to walk. Only the important guys, whites, take the train. I've worked underground since 1978 and there is more respect between black and white than before. There is no master/servant relationship now. Safety is better and always discussed.

- Now, with democracy, my cousin is a soldier to protect us all – not just the whites. That means a lot. However, unemployment is a big problem for the young. I got my matric (school leaving certificate) in 2002, but because of circumstances, I cannot find a job. I would like to study to be an electrical engineer.

- I was an international banker and was in the United States. In 1994, I returned to SA. I felt a moral obligation to come back and I now run a distribution business. Things have been difficult. There are still barriers for blacks who are not viewed as capable and competent businessmen.

- Large corporations are not interested in helping black empowerment, opportunities are opening up but there are still big gaps between black and white. The reality is we are not a Rainbow Nation yet. It is a long hard road ahead.

- I am a roadside hairdresser. I use a car battery to power the clippers. I charge five rand for a shave and ten rand for a cut.

- I am of the 'born frees' – the generation of South Africans that have grown up in the country's fledgling democracy. For the older generation of South Africans, the freedom has failed to deliver on expectations.

- In the post-apartheid era, young people have big dreams.

- People used to suffer a lot. I was a colored. Now I am a South African. Once I was nobody. Nobody now tells me what to do.

- I think Africans are better off now. I think the government is doing all right. It is doing what it can.

- Now they are oppressing whites

- The government listens to people, not like the previous one.

- People are free to do their own thing. Before, whites forced you to be a criminal.

- Racism still exists. If you go to a shop and it is a white person serving when you give money you do not give it hand-to-hand; you have to put it down on the table.

- The police have to be 80% black because of affirmative action so they do not respond to whites.

- The struggle for freedom and equality fuelled by the legally entrenched injustice system of Apartheid has lost its momentum.

- White people have separate schools and churches. They segregate themselves from blacks.

- It is an old truism that South Africa is a land of two realities. It has never been more than a short drive from lush gardens and shopping malls to the tin shanties and open sewers.

- In the sandy streets of Cape Town's Nyanga Township, an elderly man grumbled that the government was doing nothing to stop crime and unemployment – but added that he would vote for the African National Congress because he had always been an ANC man, and he was now too old to change.

- The politicians come and make promises, and then we will not see them for another five years. It is a common complaint.

- University education, which costs on average 13,000 rand (£1,100/$1,900) a year is out of the reach of most black South Africans.

- Where things have not changed – where people remain unemployed or live in terror of crime, there is a deep skepticism whether any political party has either the ability or the will to do anything about it.

- I am not a pessimist. The good thing is that the old oppression has gone.

- We are all equal now as citizens. We are free and there is hope.

- Change takes a long time. We do not expect miracles. Real change may not happen until the generation after us, but we are positive about the future.

- Everyone can speak their mind now.

- I have a white girlfriend. Younger ages don't really react. Older people may give odd stares. This is the best time to kiss your girlfriend!

- I would bring the Lord into people's lives. Then everyone's lives will be better.

CHAPTER 18

"Animals have Few Rights but they Have Every Right to be Here."

– Antony Douglas Williams

Friends invited us to spend a long weekend at their cottage near Margate about twenty miles from Durban on the South-East-Coast of Natal. Our hosts were expecting other guests too. The Margate I remembered was the seaside town of my childhood in Kent, England, where on its sandy beaches I turned out perfect sand castles from my plastic bucket which my annoying younger brother knocked down. Margate, England, was where crowds from London flocked during a surprise three week heat-wave. At other times this was the Margate where English holidaymakers shivered defiantly under umbrellas braving out the wind and rain in make belief it was the French Riviera.

The White Man's Burden

The Margate in South Africa was very different. Here were pristine white beaches, the bluest of blue skies, not a rain cloud in sight, not a puff of wind, sunshades, holidaymakers slathered in suntan lotion, taking care to avoid mosquitoes, the more adventurous riding the massive rollers of the warm Indian Ocean taking care to avoid stingrays or sharks.

We were looking forward to the rendezvous with our hosts at the cottage. We reckoned on an eight hour drive in total – long, very long. The N2 from Johannesburg to Durban was a four-lane fast highway and, once again, we took advantage of the roadside picnic tables provided. The N2 followed the coastline to Durban and was a pretty route. From Port Shepstone we encountered the first of many crossing herds of antelope and the highway became more rural, opening onto veldt and forest. The tall trees frequently obscured the sunlight. The further we went, the more deep and dense became the forest. Several times we questioned ourselves were we on the right trail, all seemed so endless. The trees thinned to allow patches of blue sky to peak through. In time, the forest gave way to earthy trails and later to a paved road. This was the cue to read our written instructions, turn left at the bridge, right at the sixth tree along and left again at the mealie stand. A mile or so on in the distance was a white chimney. As the white chimney drew closer, we saw a lone cottage, a one story with an attic. Driving up the gravel pathway to the cottage door from somewhere near we heard the ripple of a waterfall. Tucked into this remote corner of Natal, was a basic rustic cottage, a second home, a place of quiet and tranquility.

We were told the front door would be open; nobody locked doors in the forests of Natal. On arrival, all was quiet, too quiet.

The White Man's Burden

There was no one on the ground floor. I took the stairs to say hi and discovered our hosts and their other guests had taken to their beds. They had gone down with some sort of tummy bug the day before. They were taking each other's temperatures and the patient with the lowest temperature was the designated tea-maker. It was a sad situation. So sick were they all, I think we could have made a hasty departure and no one would have noticed but that would have been unconscionable. As a family, we rarely succumbed to colds and we prided ourselves on our good immune systems so we would take our chances and do what we could for these sick people, at the very least liquids and dry toast.

We were overwhelmingly ready to eat and our sick friends upstairs could not face food. Logic would say that if our hosts were expecting fifteen guests to a cottage so remote in the jungle, there should be food somewhere. In a tropical environment, it is more than ever important to cool or freeze food and the fridge seemed a likely place to look. I opened the fridge door and immediately took a quick jump back. Looking out at me was one large opaque eye, the eye of the largest fish I had ever seen. The fish was pushed into a shelf in arc-like fashion, the head touching one wall, the tail, the other. What it weighed, I had no idea but if I took a guess, around 30 lbs. It was huge, fat and heavy. We reckoned it was a large tuna, freshly fished from the ocean.

I had never cooked a fish this size. I think our hosts would probably have put it on the BBQ for a braai but the BBQ we found was kind of old and we had no idea how it would function. There was a stove with an oven. Could we get the fish into the oven? Would we have to cut it in half to do so? Certainly, it would have to be disemboweled and its head and tail removed. The kids and

The White Man's Burden

Philip were revolted at the thought of taking out the innards so I was deputed to perform the ghoulish task. I required a sharp knife to hack through the fish carcass and with the chef de kitchen upstairs vomiting into a bucket; I had to find it myself. I found no sharp knife. What I did find was a hacksaw.

I had been looking forward to a weekend of being pampered. Now the irony was I was doing the pampering. There were fifteen people in the cottage to eat off that fish though I doubted those upstairs would want to eat today. Oh well, c'est la vie. Spread out like lace doilies, pumpkins were growing in the yard in profusion. Therefore, tonight the menu would be tuna and pumpkin. The hacksaw made a helpful implement for both the tuna and pumpkin. We split two pumpkins and put the four halves into the oven to soften up. We then removed the softened skins from the pumpkin and put the deseeded flesh into a bowl. I had never cooked pumpkin; it was not a flavor I liked. I remembered the taste that first night at Pytchley Road when Virginia had cooked pumpkin. Pumpkin is one of those foods which is, as they say, "an acquired taste." In the 1970s, I cannot ever remember a pumpkin in Britain.

Without its head and tail, we were able, just, to get the fish into the oven. Two hours later, five starving guests sat down to cooked tuna – even the pumpkin was good. As anticipated, nobody upstairs joined us for dinner that night. Next day, our hosts, looking somewhat green round the gills, were sufficiently recovered to help in the kitchen. We braaied on scrumptious steaks, salad and ate assorted tropical fruits. Who knew there was ice cream?

The night of the big fish, our family went to bed pretty pooped. As I lay looking up at the ceiling before turning the light off, I saw ant after ant – an endless procession of ants trailing up the wall to my left, crossing the ceiling above my head and making their way down the wall to my right, a line of soldiers assumedly crossing the floorboards under the bed then up to the wall to my left to repeat the whole exercise. I was nervous that, while I was sleeping, ants would drop off the ceiling on to my bed. I watched for a long time but they seemed secure in their climbing. I wondered how it is that ants can climb walls and cross ceilings and not fall off. Surely the force of gravity applies to ants too or is gravitational force relative to weight? Questions like this intrigue me. Many moons ago, I wondered how do chickens mate. Nobody then knew the answer or even seemed to have thought of the question. How do male and female poultry mate when the rooster does not seem to be provided with the appropriate apparatus? Look it up.

I am dealing with ants and gravity. Ants have two sets of climbing tools on their feet; one is a suction pad and the other, tiny claws which latch on to rough surfaces. My GPS in the car sticks by suction pad to the dashboard. A spot of lick provides the vacuum to seal it. There are lots of rough places on walls and ceilings for tiny things to put hooks and suction pads into. Think of it as rock climbing when humans use crampons for foot holds. Apparently, sometimes ants do lose their foothold and fall. I just prayed these were all expert mountaineers particularly experienced at night climbing!! Nicely and politely I mentioned the ants to my host next day. She said she would pop into Margate and buy a spearmint plant, place four or five leaves around and under the bed posts which would stop the ants from crawling up to the bed and she hoped the walls. She would also wash the bed sheets in cold water with no detergent because ants are attracted to smell.

The White Man's Burden

Breakfast time, I came down to the kitchen to find we had been invaded. Three small monkeys were sitting on the kitchen counter, black-faced monkeys with long tails. We learned later they were Vervet Monkeys. The monkeys were scavengers and hung round the cottage when humans were about. They sat on the roof waiting for opportunities to enter an open window to steal food. In South Africa, Vervet Monkeys are regarded as pests, vermin. Pests or not, I found them cute. In our kitchen, they were having breakfast! Cute or not, we were in a remote place and had to value our food supplies so we were careful to make sure food items were not left out on counter-tops but put away in cupboards or fridge. Next day, Nicholas had much fun interacting with the monkeys in the grounds who were very friendly and loved to chew locally growing sugar cane he cut for them.

The Transvaal Snake Park and the Lion Park were two tourist attractions in the Johannesburg area in the 1970s. So popular was the Transvaal Snake Park with the children that we went many times. The big magnet was the exciting live snake presentations when venomous snakes were 'milked' to extract the venom for anti-venin. The trained staff allowed visitors to handle a snake that is those that wanted to. We have a photo of Nicholas with a python curled around him. The python is not a venomous snake but if it decides it really loves you, it can hug you to death!

South Africa's native snakes are some of the most venomous in Africa – among them the black and green Mamba and the Boomslang. The 'milking' is a very dangerous procedure. Milking has to be done by very expert snake handlers who know the exact pressure point to press for the snake to open its jaws and dribble the poison into a waiting cup. The biggest snake is the Python which can grow to thirty feet or more. The thickest snake is the Anaconda which can grow to forty-four inches round, likely obese on the human body mass index. We learned Cobras are faster learners than other snakes; able to tell the difference between their trainer and tourists. There are, of course, non-poisonous snakes. As frightening as they are, boas, pythons, bullsnakes and kingsnakes are not venomous. That's the good news, the bad news is these snakes have sharp teeth and a bite will cause infection. The advice from the snake handlers at the Transvaal Snake Park was to leave snakes alone just like all wildlife. Sound practical advice but when you are living in South Africa where native pythons, boas, mambas and cobras can pop up at any time and you just want to run, DON'T–standperfectly still!!

We finally, not very enthusiastically, took a visit to the Johannesburg Lion Park. After the long weekend in the Kruger National Park among nature in the raw, there was no zoo or Animal Park to match that experience. The Lion Park is a man-made safari where tourists drive through and make believe they are up close and personal with the king of the jungle, ferocious and fierce, ready waiting to pounce and consume them when, in fact, the lions are lazy, sleepy, old, domesticated cats, fed twice a day on kibble. At the entry gate, there were signs advising patrons not to open car doors or windows in the park. We heard odd shuffles on the roof of the car. We could see monkeys and baboons on the roof of the car ahead and this was obviously the same on our car roof. Long, hairy arms dangled down the front windscreen and over the rear car window. Nicholas took it upon himself to defy the park rules, wound down the rear seat window an inch or two, just sufficient for a nosey baboon to take a nip at his finger. A rather pale-faced and subdued son found himself at the Park's First Aid Post for a tetanus shot, antiseptic and a bandaid.

The White Man's Burden

This was the third time Nicholas had been in trouble with his finger. The first was pre-kindergarten in a retail carpet store. In the carpet store, there was a rotating rolodex display of carpet samples. Nicholas put his finger in between the samples. A blood-curdling scream resonated throughout the store. I rushed to pull the finger out rather too quickly. The end of the finger is particularly fleshy and prone to bleed profusely and it did, leaving a trail of blood on the shop floor. With a hyperventilating, terrified, wide-eyed child, sticking a dripping bloody finger into my face, I was embarrassed at the trail of blood we were leaving which in no way could I help clean up. My car was parked right outside the store but Nicholas continued to scream and I was unable to calm him down to drive to the Emergency Hospital. I asked a sales person in the carpet store to call a taxi. Hemoglobin in the blood acts as a binder when it hits the air and binds with the fibers in carpets and car seats. The floor of the carpet store was a mess. The back seat of the taxi was a mess. As we exited the taxi and paid the fare, I do not think the taxi driver was aware of the bloodied back seat. I can well imagine to this day there are traces of Nicholas's DNA in the store and the back seat of the taxi. The second time was on his first day at school when he was five, he came home with a bandaged finger. He had poked his finger into the classroom hamster cage giving the hamster a tasty lunch. To date, Nicholas still has eight fingers and two thumbs.

Animals are beautiful people. Looked at in this way the popular conception of animals as violent gorgers at the ready to devour the next four legged creature fades into... well, if you were hungry you would kill to eat. Poachers shoot elephants and rhinos for their tusks, horns and hides. Wild life sanctuaries were created to be safe, impenetrable to illegal hunters, except they are not.

The White Man's Burden

Where money is concerned, there are no limits to what man will do and markets will be found. The numbers of rhinos and elephants lessen every year. The Kruger National Park was thought to be unassailable with its rigorous precautions. However, the Kruger is not immune and can be targeted just as other African wildlife parks. That there might be a future without these magnificent beasts is beyond comprehension but there lurks the possibility.

Recently while walking the trails of Rithets Bog, a small natural habitat in an urban development in Victoria, Canada, I saw a mother duck with nine little ducklings. Hubby duck was on parent duty nearby. I believe ducks mate for life. I had with me my four-month old puppy, Guinness, for whom it was her first sight of a duck not to mention the nine ducklings. Guinness was off leash. She stood in wonderment. She made no move. It crossed my mind she was remembering the mother she left just two weeks earlier. Animals are more than fight or flight; they are lovers, parents, children, elders. Elephants mourn the passing of a family member and have closely related sisterhoods. A young man bought a lion cub from Harrods, London in the days before restrictions on exotic animals. His plan was to keep the lion in his basement until it was almost a year old and then to release it into a rehabilitation park in Africa. He did this. Two years later, he returned to the exact spot in the rehabilitation park where he had left the cub. Out of the wild emerged Christian, a magnificent, full grown lion. They embraced like two old friends, big hugs and friendly sparring. We underestimate the emotions, intelligence and spirituality of the animal world. Long may South Africa's beasts continue wild and free.

CHAPTER 19

The Rainbow Nation

Canada is the first country to legislate an official policy of multi-culturalism, a mosaic of ethnic cultures, Sikh, Muslim, Italian, Greek, Chinese, where all cultures co-exist in peace and harmony. It is not the melting pot system in which immigrants are encouraged to assimilate into the way of life of the new country of residence. In Canada, it is possible to retain ethnic identity and also be Canadian. The small cul-de-sac in Mississauga where we lived as new immigrants to Canada was a veritable United Nations of peoples, red dots, turbans, saris, niqabs and hijabs.

While Canada has good-natured multiplurism, South Africa was breaking every rule in the book in regard to human rights with its brutal regime of white racial superiority. Though the Western world loudly voiced its condemnation of Apartheid, there was not much they could do other than to express horror, impose trade sanctions and insist on mixed-race international sports to which South Africa defiantly replied "no".

In the late 1980s, there were rumors of secret conversations taking place in Cape Town. The National Government was quietly listening. The consequences of isolation, rejection, condemnation were hurting trade, South Africa's identity as a sovereign nation and international sport. Major companies hastened to take their interests out of South Africa wanting not to be tainted with racism. What spurred the Afrikaner National Government's change of heart? Was it embarrassment? Was it trade sanctions? Considered an unstable market, investors were holding back because of possible eruptions, uprisings, even civil war. Was it isolation? South Africa's white artists were banned from performing in other countries and major entertainers refused to work in South Africa – or was it the sports boycott? In sports, Apartheid raised its ugly head and South Africa refused to field inter-racial teams. South Africans are naturals at sport. The cut-off from international sport had a big impact on both black and white. Some say it was the sports sanctions that were the straw that finally broke the camel's back.

The world is much more global today. Granted there is instability in the Middle East but the coming of the Internet has changed the world forever. The internet enables transparency, country to country; human rights violations no longer remain unseen, unheard. In Tahrir Square that Sunday, there were mobile phones, TV cameras and in the blink of an eye, the whole world knew about the uprising in Egypt and the Arab Spring. Had social media been more advanced in the '80s and '90s, it is possible South Africans and the world would have been better placed to bring more pressure for change?

It was in the 1980's that the ball started rolling when Nelson Mandela sent letters to President F.W. De Klerk outlining ways to peaceful resolution. Mr. De Klerk with the cool calm of a canny businessman came to a realization that the Western World was in a new era of intercultural sensitivity enacted in multiculturalism or the more trendy phrase 'community cohesion'. Mr. De Klerk knew full well that the prejudice of Apartheid was out of sync with this modernism and its continuance would destroy South Africa. In effect, racial segregation was a losing game not just in international sports but in economics and prosperity and in South Africa's status as a leader of African States. If South Africa was to survive as an economic power, it had to be on the same page as the rest of the world.

The change had to be made quietly and clandestinely. Four years of negotiation went on with Nelson Mandela and the South African Intelligence to explore any commonality between the two parties. For convenience and comfortable discussion, Mandela was moved from Robben Island to the more upscale Pollsmoor Prison near Cape Town. This time there was no invitation to afternoon tea from Nelson Mandela to Mr. De Klerk as there was to Rugby Captain, Francois Pienaar.

For many years there has been talk in Canada about reforming the Senate, its Upper House of Parliament, even to abolishing it. Such a major constitutional change involves obtaining agreement from each of the Provinces and the Territories, a complex feat. In South Africa, it was the eleven tribes that voiced their needs loud and clear. The Inkatha Freedom Party, running a close second to the African National Congress, took a firm stand for its own political policies as did the King of Kwa-Zulu for his throne. The Government and Nelson Mandela assured the Qua-Zulu King he would retain his monarchy and made concessions to the Inkatha

Freedom Party. The final obstacles to peace were the Afrikaner extremists. Clause after clause, revision after revision and detail upon detail were deleted, added, changed, re-written until agreement slowly took shape.

At the end of four years of finding middle ground, Nelson Mandela was released from jail. There were other well-known figures involved in the negotiations too, US's Henry Kissinger and UK Foreign Secretary Lord Carrington. Thus, South Africa's change to democracy was not a sudden conversion but a well thought out plan. It was only at the completion of this process that the World heard the public announcement of the proposed democratic election giving each and every South African a vote. Interestingly this was the only time in world history that a nation has changed from one political system to another without civil war. Apartheid officially ended in 1994 when the African National Congress won the first election and South Africa took its seat in the United Nations General Assembly after a 20-year absence.

> *"What is taking place in South Africa is such a deed – a deed resounding over the earth — a deed of peace. It brings hope to all South Africans. It opens new horizons for Sub-Saharan Africa. It has the capacity to unlock the tremendous potential of our country and our region. The new era which is dawning in our country, beneath the great southern stars, will lift us out of the silent grief of our past and into a future in which there will be opportunity and space for joy and beauty – for real and lasting peace."*

F. W. De Klerk, Nobel Lecture, 1993.

The White Man's Burden

In Western countries, grumbles continue to be heard about voter lethargy, small turnouts for political elections. That day, 17th April, 1994, in South Africa's first democratic election, there were no complaints as nineteen million votes were counted, no black or colored man had ever marked an 'X' on a voting slip or slipped a vote into a ballot box. When the results were tallied, the African National Congress held the majority. The night of the ANC win, the night of the change to democracy, was a night of wild jubilation, of overwhelming emotions, partying well into the small hours. It had taken over forty-six years but, unbelievably the dream had come true. The dream was so much more than 'one man one vote'; it was the official abolition of legal racism. To a black or colored South African, it meant being a persona grata, free to live how and where he wished, in dignity and respect, free to attain goals, free to hold his head up high. It is a good, wholesome feeling to own your self-worth, to be proud of your identity, to say, "I am me."

It was anticipated that after the change to democracy, South Africa would become a power house on the world stage of industry, commerce and technology, except that having the vote did not turn the country into the anticipated fairyland. Canadians put much faith in having democracy and having the vote. Yet in Canada there is still child poverty and homelessness. There are those who say too much emphasis on the free vote is not a sure recipe for equality.

A South African friend now living in Canada remarked to me that the only difference between South Africa under Apartheid and South Africa in democracy is the right for a person to individually, without coercion, elect a government. Other than that not much is different. "Whites" he said "continue to make the money and blacks continue to be employed by whites," and this opinion is echoed by discontented blacks who maintain whites still run the economy, still have the best houses, the best jobs and continue to benefit from a domestic worker system entrenched in black history. Some black South Africans maintain that white South Africans are still subversively 'for' Apartheid, though in the majority sense this is far from the case.

Black women are now black Madams. In the kitchen, there is black Nelly making afternoon tea for the black Madam. However, shortage of employment, lack of skills and education, and a legacy of domestic service, still sees black domestic workers as domestic helps for white South Africans except now there is a trade off. Nelly is protected by the Union of South African Domestic Service and Allied Workers. She comes to work from her own home, can work part-time, place her children in regulated day care, and has running water, in-house toilets, electricity, television, a washing machine and a home which, though modest, is comfortable. There is a minimum wage and rules that domestics should work no more than forty-five hours a week and not more than nine hours a day. On Sundays or public holidays, there is double pay. Employers who have live-in domestic staff deduct ten percent for accommodation for which there are defined standards. Domestics get severance pay, one week for each year of service, as well as four months' unpaid maternity leave. If the home help works for more than twenty-four hours a month, she receives Employment Insurance still termed in the negative 'Unemployment Insurance.' Madams can no longer fire an employee on a whim, "Eish, I've got a lazy one this time." There has to be just cause such as proven stealing.

The relationship between the black Madam and the black domestic is different to the white *baas* arrangement. Often Nelly is the older of the two and assumes a more motherly role. In black culture, elders are venerated which makes it difficult for a younger black madam to delegate or instruct a senior domestic worker. No matter what your status, you show respect to the elders. "Please clean the second bedroom today" becomes a wish that is completed on the domestic's terms and then only if she it thinks necessary. The white Madam, generalized as working her black maid too hard, too long, a stern employer without compassion, is now the black Madam spoken of in terms of unreasonableness, arrogance, a cut above her station, even terror.

Apartheid to blame for blackouts – Zuma

13 December 2014 9:12

President Jacob Zuma. Picture: Siphiwe Sibeko/Reuters

President Jacob Zuma says South Africa's energy problems were a product of apartheid and government was not to blame for the current blackouts.

"The problem [is] the energy was structured racially to serve a particular race, not the majority," Zuma told delegates at the Young Communist League's congress in Cape Town yesterday.

He said the ANC had inherited the power utility from the previous regime which had only provided electricity to the white minority.

The White Man's Burden

The change to democracy has had its effect on low-income white South Africans whose jobs are now held by black workers. It is the black resume that jumps the queue. In some ways, it is black superiority and smacks of reverse Apartheid. Apartheid is a bad memory that whites would like to forget and white unemployment does not make the headlines.

Is there a future for the white South African in a democratic black South Africa? For those who are flexible, those who are able to adjust to fit in, there is certainly a future. It is fortunate that the Rainbow Nation is a forgiving one. For those die-hard white Afrikaners stuck in their own reality and unable to change, there are no guarantees.

There has been much reported in world media about violence and mass crime in post-Apartheid South Africa. History repeats itself and the catalysts, as everywhere, are poverty, poor parenting, unstable housing and poor education. White or black, a man's self-esteem is defined by his job and his financial contribution to the family. Unemployment adds to male frustration. The quick remedy, a purse snatch, a store robbery or worse!

The escalation of petty crime leaves homeowners under constant threat. Under Apartheid, most white house owners had an alarm system and a guard dog. Now it is black-owned houses with such safeguards. Career criminals are everywhere, organized attacks on commercial and retail centers, ATM bombings, and attacks on armored cars.

White Afrikaners, landowners and farmers, are no longer able to take advantage of cheap labor as under Apartheid. Whether it is revenge or greed, farmers are at particular risk from black insurgents who murder and pillage these easy targets in remote and isolated locations. If there is someone today who lives with a gun under his pillow, it is the white Afrikaner farmer.

Criticism of corruption and bribery are leveled at African National Congress politicians said to be enriching themselves through awarding government contracts to personal connections. The political world everywhere seems to invite scandal. In South Africa, there was the Travelgate scandal; forty members of parliament were found to have illegally used parliamentary travel vouchers worth eighteen million rand for personal use. President Zuma and his family unduly benefited from a R215 million security upgrade to their property for work estimated at R36 million. South Africa is a fledgling nation in terms of politics and democracy. Canada, the elder statesman at 150 years old, still has political scandals, the Liberal Party sponsorship in Quebec, robocalls to confuse voters in the 2011 election, and the 2014 Senate scandal of misappropriated expenses.

Signs of the influence of British history are fading. The iconic red mail pillar-box can be bought on EBay, the British store Marks and Spencer closed. F.W. Woolworth proliferates, not as the original five-and-dime store, but as a full service copy of all that Marks & Spencer stood for, goodies that appeal to the white English South African. Brits who lived through Apartheid say they have a sense of loss of the familiar, of privilege, of role. In truth, their loss is shattered delusions.

Prior to 1976, the Apartheid Government resisted the introduction of television fearing its content would dilute the state's control and misguide its citizens. Television had been going just two years when we arrived. Why we decided to go without television in 1978/9 was because there was only one television channel. Now, black television anchors read the news. Today, there are multi English channels including community television. The state-owned South African Broadcasting Company has three channels and television channels broadcast in all thirteen official languages.

I looked up some current programming. Surprise, there were the UK and USA old soaps, 'Dallas', "Days of our Lives', 'The Young and the Restless'. 'Desperate Housewives' struck me as an ironic satire of the white South African Madam. 'Law and Order' was again paradoxical in terms of the current criminal situation in South Africa. There is homemade programming too, an Afrikaans drama, 'Skeletons in the Closet,' featuring psychiatrists balancing careers with family and patients.

To have SABC 2, requires a license, a carryover from the BBC. SABC 2 seems to be the channel for breaking news and World news but also has original South African programming. One channel is showing a mini-series about King Shaka Zulu and his adventures with the British traders in the 1800s. There is reality television, 'The Ultimate Braai Master' described as a competition to win a fifty-two day culinary adventure. There is the South African Film and Television Awards, the 2015 South African Person of the Year Awards and the South African Beauty Pageant featuring none other than Donald Trump. There is a sitcom about the white Madam, and her black maid, Eve, a spoof on relationships between the white baas and black maid under one roof.

South Africans have by-passed the land line to the cell phone. Almost twenty-five million South Africans have access to the Internet. It is as usual to see a bus load of strap-hanging cell phone users in South Africa as in New York. Education too is in the technological age, entire classrooms now one-on-one digital.

The argument to ring in the new and ring out the old is strong. There are changes to city names and public holidays. White Afrikaners assert that public holidays commemorating figures of the past have nothing to do with racial dynamics – are just history. Black South Africans hold contrary opinion that the battles won by the Voortrekkers over the Zulus were a triumph of race over race with the white race prevailing, a prediction of eventual white supremacy.

The trauma of racial discrimination and white superiority that impacted the black peoples of South Africa has given rise to some thoughtful sharing and repairing initiatives. These innovations are profound and meaningful, new in concept, humanitarian in effect, to include all South African citizens. Statutory holidays are Human Rights Day, Freedom Day, Workers Day, National Women's Day, Day of Reconciliation, Day of Goodwill, Mandela Day. Jan Smuts Airport, where we first set foot on South African soil, is now Johannesburg's O.R. Tambo International Airport. The name change is to eradicate an Afrikaner statesman in favor of a new hero, Apartheid freedom fighter, Oliver Reginald Tambo, fondly known as 'O.R', a President of the African National Congress for thirty years.

In 1994, a new National Anthem was sung "Nkosi Sikelel iAfrika" – God Bless Africa. The lyrics were taken from the five most widely spoken of South Africa's thirteen official languages – Xhosa (first stanza, first two lines), Zulu (first stanza, last two lines), Sesotho (second stanza), Afrikaans (third stanza), and English (final stanza). The old National Anthem was 'Die Stem van Suid-Afrika'; in English 'The Call of South Africa.' Again, there has been much thought given to making South Africa one nation.

A quick update on the Kruger National Park, it now has a kosher kitchen. Game drives followed by Gefilte fish and Latkes before lion tracking, Shabbos in the Bush!

As recently as 2015, Cape Town student demonstrations brought down one of the last remnants of Apartheid, the decades-old statue of British Colonialist, Cecil Rhodes. Demonstrations began with a student flinging excrement at the bronze sculpture and students climbing into the statue's base singing anti-apartheid songs. On the internet, a petition read, "More than a statue, the statue has great symbolic power; it glorifies a mass-murderer who exploited black labor and stole land from indigenous people." Cecil Rhodes was a businessman, a politician and a philanthropist. His legacy to education, the prestigious Rhodes scholarship (now the Mandela Rhodes Scholarship) sent and continues to send, thousands of international students to Oxford University, England. Notable Rhodes Scholars have been Bill Clinton, Canadian Prime Minister John Turner and Canadian Broadcasting's Rex Murphy. In Pretoria, a smaller Afrikaner counter-campaign, called 'Rhodes Must Stay,' argued that the statue should be protected as a symbol of South Africa's heritage. The very Afrikaner Pretoria had volunteers chained to the memorial statue of Paul Kruger to keep it safe. It still stands.

The White Man's Burden

Since democracy in 1994, the South African Government steers away from any type of nationalism preferring to acknowledge each culture and tradition as unique and integral to the pride of individual loyalty to the Rainbow State. With thirteen official languages, it is possible to be, for example, a Zulu South African, a Xhosa South African, a white Afrikaner South African, Indian, Chinese and Japanese South African.

Comparisons have been made between Nazi Germany and Apartheid. Both excluded populations from living in certain areas, doing certain jobs, entering certain businesses. Apartheid South Africa was in no way innocent of torture and violence, but there was no attempt at mass extermination. While staying at an International Hostel, I got to talk with young German students. Some expressed the view that National Socialism, in its pure state, was a good idea but badly carried out. Some South Africans believe Apartheid as a system was not inherently bad, but badly carried out. The German students were vibrantly enthusiastic about their own and their nation's future, had confidence their leaders were carefully watchful for signs of emerging nationalism. These young Germans, who learned their country's history from school textbooks, feel this is another era much as we English feel about the medieval age of witches burning at the stake or beheading the wife because she could not birth a male heir. Some students felt there will always be a sense of lingering collective guilt.

There are those who do not want to tear down remnants of Afrikaner past; who wish the names of streets or statues such as Lydenburg (Place of Suffering), Vryheid (Place of Freedom), Pietermaritzburg, (named after the famous Voortrekker leader), Pilippolis, Bethulie, (named after the Boers' beloved Bible), to remain as reminders of history and past mistakes. In wanting their nation to be free of the shame of its baggage, there are those who fear forgetting past mistakes is a danger of repeating them.

Is race still an issue in the new South Africa? Race is an issue in every country for the singular reason race is about fear of difference, and fear is an innate human emotion. Fear of difference is weakened with familiarity and education. When racial customs and traditions interrelate, when each comes to know the other's humanity, there is a common sameness, goodness, and feeling. To feel that sense of togetherness, alikeness, compatibility, groups of different colors locate together, whether in ghettos, stomping grounds or neighborhoods. Caucasians too locate in togetherness. It is that sense of togetherness that provides community for groups of different skin colors, eye shapes, languages. That South Africa's major cities remain largely in black and white neighborhoods, that in London, England, the suburbs of Brixton and Southall are the domains of West and East Indians respectively, that in British Columbia, Canada, Sikhs abound in Surrey, Chinese in Richmond, that Italians abound in Little Italy, Toronto, that Greektown road signs are dual-language, Greek and Canadian, that Italians prevail in New York, is community living, multiculturalism and how it works best for cultures. A few years ago in Toronto, black crime, gangs and violence were escalating to serious proportions. The Toronto School Board took an unusual decision – to open an African Canadian only elementary school. There was strong dissension from some black parents maintaining their kids would miss out not being in mainstream school. However, school marks from the African Canadian elementary school were the highest ever and importantly the crime rate went down dramatically. There are now three all black schools in Toronto, two primary and a high school.

The White Man's Burden

Black South Africans have a mixed tradition of stories from ancestry, witch doctors, sorcery, voodoos, good and evil spirits, folklore and curing remedies. It would be a big loss to the world if these rich traditions were to vanish into the melting pot. Hopefully, the era of multiculturism will maintain individual traditions while intermingling for friendship, intermarrying, inter-partnering with the mixed races ever evolving into a wider world. As South Africans embrace concepts of Western living and the technological age, the loss of tradition becomes a risk but I think an unlikely risk.

An odd event emerged after we left South Africa. Philip had picked up some South African music cassettes wanting to get the feel of South African music. On his way to work or on the way home, he would pop a cassette into the car tape deck. One of the cassettes, labeled Cold Fact, featured an American male singer guitarist called Sixto Rodriguez with original songs, many of which we would now call protest songs. Listening to his album, there was a smidgeon of early Rap (though Rap was not known at the time), rhyming poetry and I found it somewhat reminiscent of Leonard Cohen. Rodriguez' voice was rich, easy listening, pleasant, emotional, and moving, above all, every word was clear. In 2016, I watched a documentary about Rodriguez. Apparently, his attempts to market his records in 1970s America went nowhere. A bootlegged copy of his Cold Fact recording found its way to South Africa. The lyrics struck a chord with black South Africans in the era of Apartheid. The words bore no relevance to racism but they were about the fight for people's rights in poor inner cities. Incredibly, in South Africa, Rodriguez became a cult, more popular than Elvis Presley.

The White Man's Burden

Over the next two decades, Rodriguez became a household name in South Africa but totally unknown in any other country and unknown to Rodriguez. Cold Fact went platinum. There was rumor Rodriguez had committed suicide setting himself on fire before an audience. Two South African promoters were intrigued about a singer rock star adulated in South Africa but unknown anywhere else and determined to find out more about him. After a long search, they got a lead to a small record promoter in the US and found out that Rodriguez was alive and well, living in Detroit. He had been working at a humble job in construction for 40 years, married with a wife, three children and grandchildren, but totally unaware of his success in South Africa. Subsequently, Rodriguez went to South Africa several times and played to sold out concerts. If you are wondering about his first name, "Sixto," it is because he was the sixth child in his family. The documentary "Searching for Sugarman" won an Oscar.

There are people born after the dismantling of Apartheid who know nothing of how it was to struggle under a racially segregated system. How will the story be played out in the school-rooms of South Africa? Can the South African school system develop the topic to be a lesson of civic identity, citizenship, national and constitutional values, a lesson in understanding and forgiveness; that such tragedies occur, that society's thinking is ever-evolving, that optimism is a better message than hatred? It will be difficult to get past the image of hatred but as said before I, personally, found the black nation a forgiving one. I am hoping those who teach Apartheid as history will find a way.

America had slavery. Germany had racism. England had imperialism. Canada has only just acknowledged and made public apology for the wrongfulness done to its peoples of the First Nations. I hope in Canadian schoolrooms, we, too, will be honest enough to tell the new generations the true story of Canada's guilt. There is much to tell and it needs to be told. How to do so with compassion and wisdom is not difficult, if the will is there.

Alexandra still has large unemployment but it has decent houses with indoor toilets, running tap water, paved streets and a train station. Johannesburg is all spruced up, coffee bars, cosmopolitan restaurants, streets lined with tables serving anything from sushi to crocodile steaks, tall office towers, a Hilton or Holiday Inn, vibrant malls, a food market and a growing night-life scene, a trendy city centre of loft apartments, theatres and museums, in particular the Apartheid Museum. Gone are the litter-strewn streets, derelict stores. Decline and decay is trans-formed into a modern, trendy city, the business and tourist pulse of South Africa. In Johannesburg, there are one and a half million trees.

However, the legacy of Apartheid still remains for those who went through the Apartheid years as maids and garden boys and for those who remain unskilled. Domestic work is still the largest source of employment for black women. It is the young black woman who has seen the change. African traditional and modern designs are marketed all over the world; the black African woman adorns glossy magazine pages. She has come into her own, taken her rightful place, stunningly elegant and beautiful. African fashion, color, texture and design are much in demand by Western women. African women complete schooling, attend university and can now be found in most professions. In 2015, South African Airways announced the hiring of its first black woman pilot.

The White Man's Burden

I think it is fair to say the racial democracy Nelson Mandela fought for is solid. Fifty-five million South Africans live in racial freedom. In his Presidency, a social network for education and health was put in place. Mandela knew that not everything in the garden was rosy but in regard to human dignity, he could rightly say "mission accomplished". In place now are government initiatives previously denied to black South Africans such as clean, drinkable water, proper sanitation and welfare for the unemployed, free medical services for low-income earners or with no income at all, disability and housing grants, child-care benefits, full education and bursaries. Yet still, black South Africans complain change has not come fast enough to improve poverty once attributed to white domination. Under Apartheid, South Africa had a vibrant economy, sound investments and, economically, was the envy of the World. Under Apartheid, South Africa was the richest of the African nations.

In 2017, South Africa's economy is in crisis. Its unemployment rate at 27% is the highest in the World. In 2016, crime of all types was rampant, 34 murders per 100,000 people. There is much disapproval of the failed promises of the African National Congress and criticism for slowness to reform. Once upon a time, the reason given for the divide between rich and poor would have been squarely laid at the feet of Apartheid. In post-Apartheid, it is class that is the dividing line, nothing to do with race, more to do with education, family background and money. South Africa has the unenviable task familiar to all Western countries – how to close the ever increasing economic gap between rich and poor. The cry is that government mismanagement is the cause of unemployment and is now the black man's burden. However, playing the political blame game is a well-used tactic and a forever game. Though it is true many promises are yet to be fulfilled to improve the lot of the black South African, can it be denied that the freedom of its peoples ranks first and foremost?

It is too much to expect that the move to democracy would be a smooth ride without bumps. It will take time to get things right. The effects of Apartheid linger in a people broken by the system, a residual Post Traumatic Stress Disorder. Twenty years is not enough time to heal open wounds, to catch-up on lost self-worth, lost education and lost civil rights. It will need more than two generations of feeling good to get everything working smoothly but it will happen.

CHAPTER 20

Departure

Our four-month assignment that lengthened into two years was coming to an end. We were leaving South Africa with mixed feelings. We had been given an opportunity available to few – I had seen elephant. We had so many adventures, immeasurable, precious and unforgettable but always tainted by the face of inhumanity. We had been personal witnesses to reports in those British newspapers; the horrors were real. We had witnessed overt racism before our very eyes.

Philip and I made new and valued friendships that we were sad to leave. Our friends threw us a farewell party, cooking up traditional dishes: Potjie, Boerewors, and Sosaties on the braai. We were given leaving gifts of South African artwork, tapestry, and beads. In my office, as I write, hang pictures depicting two immensely beautiful, South African Zulu women each with a child. With hugs and tears, we promised to keep in touch. Had

Facebook been around, it would have been easy but alas all we could do was commit to sending annual Christmas cards, photographs and newsletters. The children, too, had made good friends. Nicholas was sad to leave Ralph, the steadfast friend who had come to his defense so readily and Karen, her many school friends, Cavil in particular.

Two years in a country is a long holiday. There gets to be a sense of belonging, a familiarity with the ways of the Rainbow Nation, land of eternal sun, the ugly yet beautiful insects, the bushveld, the temperate grasslands, scattered trees and savannah where roamed zebra, rhinoceros, elephant, giraffe, animals not native to any other country. We had acquired affection for the traditions and ancestral spirits of the black peoples bravely dancing their way through dire poverty. We could pronounce the names of rivers with strange sounding names, the Bamboesspruit, the Limpopo, the Tugela. We had conquered the rolling waves of the Indian Ocean, scavenged in the rock pools of Camps Bay and burnt our feet on the white sands of Umhlanga Beach. And throughout this great country, always were the lekker braais. We had seen spectacularly colored birds and butterflies, creatures great and small, all new to us. We had witnessed the traditions and cultures of the tribes of the Rainbow Nation, the Witch Doctor, the Sangoma and the Tokoloshe. We were leaving with immeasurable memories and tales to tell. In our two years, I had become a spoiled Madam but a spoiled Madam tainted by guilt that we could do nothing for a people where skin color and quality of hair determined their destiny.

It sounds so very self-indulgent to say we would miss our house staff but we would. I cannot deny I would miss a cleaner, cook, gardener, built-in nanny but the miss would be for more than that. Though it would always be a baas/Madam relationship, I like to think we were understanding, considerate employers, certainly easygoing and a connection was built that we were fond of them and they of us. At Rosemary's job interview I had made it clear to her we were temporary residents and I assured her that before we returned to England, we would make sure she was working in a new job. We advertised in the Johannesburg Star recommending our excellent maid, excellent nanny and excellent cook, a maid both efficient and cheerful. We were inundated with replies. Madams hold tight to good maids and a Madam would pounce on a recommended maid rather than an unemployed maid or even a maid with a certificate of skills from the Centre for Concern. I will miss Rosemary, her efficiency, common sense, her honesty, her commitment to her job, her face crinkling as together we had a good chuckle and, of course, her adoration of Elizabeth. As we said goodbye, I asked Rosemary, "Will you miss us?" "Yes," she said "but I will miss my baby more." It made no sense that Rosemary looked after my three children and was unable to look after her own four. In the African jungle, the mother lion purrs alongside her cubs and, only when she is sure they can manage on their own, does she let them leave the den. I will miss Philemon, that tall, solitary silhouette, that monumental fountain of the garden, so laid-back, amenable, disarming, so always ready and willing.

I would miss the cheap vegetables and fruits sold by the sack full for a rand or two. Tropical vegetables were still not freely available in 1980s England. Ships transported mainly industrial cargo then. Tropical fruits do not freeze well and would not last the voyage. As the air industry developed, names of fruits and vegetables never heard of in London such as pawpaws, papaya, mangoes, pomegranates, naartjies, granadillas, became available in British stores. I would miss fresh lemon juice squeezed from a lemon tree in the garden. Lemon juice for a recipe would have to come from the supermarket. I would have to scour the store fruit shelves for green bananas to ripen slowly.

I would particularly miss the fish. The geography of the two oceans, the cold Atlantic and the warm Indian Ocean, produced many species of fish, snapper, king clip, snoorsnoek, bas, hake, sassi, calamari, and yellow fin tuna. Seafood is prepared in many ways in South Africa. The Cape Malay Indian influence brought pickled and curried fish to the table. Traditionally, South Africans are meat eaters – steaks, Sosaties on the braai, but I also went to several fish braais. And I went to a pig roast. A whole pig was lowered into newly dug hole and fired on a bed of smoldering coals or cinders. The hole was filled in and the pig left to cook for twenty-four hours. At dinner time, our host dug the pig up, put it on a spit and carved it for serving. It was, of course, done to perfection, delicious. We would all miss going shoeless, the souls of my feet so hardened we could have walked on a bed of nails. Only at school did the kids wear shoes. However, the biggest miss would be the climate of Johannesburg and its suburbs. At 6000 feet above sea level, the weather is so very perfect, never too hot and rarely too cold. In other South African provinces, the temperature climbs sky-high, can be hot, clammy and draining.

There were some items we would not miss. I would not miss the thick, greasy battered fish and chips of Johannesburg. Fish and chips are Britain's national pride, and shop owners know how to fry fish and chips right proper! I would not miss the empty orange brown earth and the scarcity of trees at the roadsides and highways, sparse, not even a weed. I now have a much better reverence for 'England's green and pleasant land'. Oh and I forgot, I will not miss those fat, slimy, lazy, gigantic bugs smearing ooze in the hallways of the house.

As I looked at Philemon, lying in the sun sucking a straw, so blissful and carefree, it seemed to me he was the epitome of the black South African, laid-back, easy-going, happy-go-lucky, always a big round smile. It seemed to me contentment is indigenous in the temperament of the Black South African. However, Philemon had a roof over his head, a job and an easy Master. I should not generalize his happiness because there were millions of unemployed black South Africans in the townships and Homelands in dire poverty who would tell very different tales. Nevertheless, I return to my original thought, the nature of the black South African is perhaps why the calculating, driven, keen for power white man, was able to so easily override the majority nation and for so long.

The risk of civil war and bloodshed was growing ever stronger and it seemed to us that the white Afrikaner was not going to give up easily. Yet, someday, from somewhere, a Moses must come to lead black South Africa out of bondage. Fifteen years after we left South Africa that Moses did come; the miracle took place and without blood-shed. It takes only one person to make a difference and that one person had been waiting in the wings a long time.

We had considered asking South Africa to adopt us. It was the best of living for sure, if you were white. We would have a much higher standard of living here than we could ever contemplate in England. Our leaving came with a strong sense of conscience; we were walking away from those who desperately needed kindness and compassion. We could have argued that we are British, temporary residents, here to do a job and go home, that the humanity of these circumstances was not of our making and nothing to do with us; not our burden. We had an easy out. We could have stayed to support the troubled whites to be a thorn in the side of the white Afrikaner and English hearts hardened against change. As with the starfish on the beach, we could have made a difference. It was not easy to leave; to simply walk away with all kinds of justifications and excuses. We endlessly tossed around the morality of the decision we had to make. Had we been born South African, we speculated, nothing would make us leave this so violated population as had many white English South Africans. Then, we reasoned we were not South Africans and what we *would* do was theoretical, pure conjecture. The 'Winds of Change' were blowing ever more fiercely; the potential for civil war, violence and blood ever stronger. We had young children. At eighteen, Nicholas would be conscripted to the South African Defense Force. It is one thing to fight for democracy, quite another to fight for racism. Important also to us were our family ties in England. Our parents were in England. Our children would lose those special relationships with grandparents, cousins, aunts and uncles Thus, it was with conflicted and complicated feelings that we left.

We returned home, British Airways. This time Philip flew with us and it was a direct flight no stopping for fuel. That April day at Heathrow Airport, descending the ramp I felt a distinct nip in the air. The sky was grey and it seemed there could be rain any time. A typical day in England but it was home and without hesitation, I would say we were glad to return to our three-up, two-down, semi-detached. I remembered to dig out from our bags the teak wooden salad-servers with carved heads of antelope and giraffe, souvenirs we had bought in Cape Town to give to London friends and relatives.

In the warm clime of South Africa, our kids had lived largely outdoors and mainly in bare feet. Being shoed and cooped up indoors in Ealing, gave rise to antsy and argumentative behavior. Philip and I would have loved nothing better than to relax into the comfort of our living room sofa for the remaining few weeks in our London home. It was not to be. We found ourselves at the local public swimming pool, targets of long stares. We had not realized how deeply sun-tanned we were and how sharply we stood out from the pale skins of the London swimmers. April in London is not a time for suntan and the Brits in the pool likely saw us as well-off folks recently returned from two weeks in Majorca. They were not far out, of course; just wrong place and wrong perception.

Friends and relatives expressed interest in the children's school time in South Africa. They asked the children how school differed from British school and if they had enjoyed school there. The children replied, "We loved having the whole afternoon off and no homework."

When it came to the children expressing their views on schooling in South Africa, I knew our frequent talks about Apartheid and its impact on black people had hit the mark. Now that they could freely say their piece, they launched into veritable onslaught of chatter about how glad they were to be a white family; the next time they met people with a black skin they would be twice as nice. They told how there were white children only at their school; that black children did not get to go to school – how school was free for white children but black parents had to pay and how unfair it was. They told how Afrikaner white boys taunted black kids calling them disgusting names like 'craylas' or 'jambos' and parroted their parents calling black men 'kaffir boy'. They spoke of times when they had witnessed white people being rude to servants. How at sleepovers in the homes of school friends, they had witnessed the Madam hurling a stream of brutal words at the maid for omitting a table fork. Generally when friends and relatives asked was racism as awful as the media portrayed, I let the children answer and it was an emphatic "yes."

Mention was made of the children's quite strong South African accents. Being with the kids on a day-to-day basis, their change of accent had somehow by-passed me. My mother-in-law who last heard a distinctly London British accent, now said she had difficulty understanding the children's South African accents. Family and friends were interested to hear the kids had to learn compulsory Afrikaans. Karen was quick to launch into a demonstration of her Afrikaans, which impressed all until it was discovered she was reciting a cake recipe!

Momma: Ek gaan 'n koek te maak	Momma: I'm going to make a cake
Mamma, kan ek help?	Mom, can I help?
Wat doen jy in die bak?	What do you put in the bowl?
Momma: Ek gaan suiker en botter en eiers by te voeg	Mom: I'm going to add sugar and butter and eggs
Wat nog?	What else?
Mamma : O, ek het vergeet om die sout	Mom: oh, I forgot the salt
Mamma, kan ek die koek in die oond?	Mom, can I put the cake in the oven?

The White Man's Burden

Ideally, had we our druthers, we would have preferred to return to live and work in London among our families and to be with my recently widowed father. However, the Company had transferred us to Scotland, a not too exciting prospect.

Scotland is starkly different from South Africa yet both, in their own way awesome in scenery and tradition. Ben Nevis, Scotland's highest mountain dispenses treacherous winter snow storms while South Africa's Drakensberg Mountain Range has temper tantrums, violent and dynamic, tropical storms. The eleven tribes of South Africa have diverse and colorful traditional wear, beadwork, pleated skirts of grass and cowhide, coils of necklaces and colorful woven scarves. Scottish clans have dashing kilts, sporrans, a dagger in a knee-high sock. The Royal Stuart clan has perhaps the brightest colors, predominantly red. Both Scotland and South Africa have heroes and battles. Bonnie Prince Charlie was defeated at Culloden Field in his attempt to secure the English throne for his father; tribal chief, Dingane came to grief at the hands of the Boers at the Battle of Blood River. Where weather overall is concerned, there is a stark difference. When the sky is clear blue in Glasgow, it is a high-pressure system and it is cold, real cold. When the sky is clear blue in Johannesburg, it is nicely not too hot, not too cold. In Glasgow, it seems forever dreary and the snow is deeper than I have ever known. We lived there a year and I recall one sunny day when the kids on our street wore swim suits! For sure, South Africa was a hard act to follow.

At the gym today, five guys were working out, four white and one black. It was guy-talk in the gym. "How many reps today, man?" "Not enough" replied the black guy. Listening to

The White Man's Burden

the conversation that day in the gym, black and white working out together, no racism, all harmony and respect, for sure it is a better world I live in.

It is 1979 and I am sitting on the stoep of our rented house in Kensington B. It is a blazing hot Christmas Day. We have all had a swim in the pool, the Giant Toad is back, the Bougainvillea is in full bloom and the lizard is still in the mailbox. Bunches of unripe bananas grow in the Atrium. Elizabeth, our baby, is cavorting in Rosemary's room off the kitchen. We all know Apartheid will not last forever.

"When there is peace in the country, the chief does not carry a shield."

AFRICAN PROVERB

CHAPTER 21

"I am an African…"

Thabo Mkebi

"I owe my being to the hills and the valleys, the mountains and the glades, the rivers, the deserts, the trees, the flowers, the seas and the ever-changing seasons that define the face of our native land.

"My body has frozen in our frosts and in our latter day snows. It has thawed in the warmth of our sunshine and melted in the heat of the midday sun. The crack and the rumble of the summer thunders, lashed by startling lightning, have been a cause both of trembling and of hope.

"The fragrances of nature have been as pleasant to us as the sight of the wild blooms of the citizens of the veld.

"The dramatic shapes of the Drakensberg, the soil-colored water of the Lekoa, iGqili no Thukela, and the sands of the Kgalagadi, have all been panels of the set on the natural stage on which we act out the foolish deeds of the theatre of our day.

"At times, and in fear, I have wondered whether I should concede equal citizenship of our country to the leopard and the lion, the elephant and the springbok, the hyena, the black mamba and the pestilential mosquito.

"A human presence among all these, a feature on the face of our native land thus defined, I know that none dare challenge me when I say – I am an African!

"I owe my being to the Khoi and the San whose desolate souls haunt the great expanses of the beautiful Cape; they who fell victim to the most merciless genocide our native land has ever seen; they who lost their lives in the struggle to defend our freedom and dependence and they who, as a people, perished in the result.

"Today, as a country, we keep an audible silence about these ancestors of the generations that live, fearful to admit the horror of a former deed, seeking to obliterate from our memories a cruel occurrence, which, in its remembering, should teach us not, and ever to be inhuman again.

"I am formed of the migrants who left Europe to find a new home on our native land. Whatever their own actions, they remain part of me. In my veins courses the blood of the Malay slaves who came from the East. Their proud dignity informs my bearing, their culture a part of my essence. The stripes they bore on their bodies from the lash of the slave master embossed on my consciousness are a reminder of what should not be done.

"I am the grandchild of the warrior men and women that Hintsa and Sekhukhune led, the patriots that Cetshwayo and Mphephu took to battle, the soldiers Moshoeshoe and Ngungunyane taught always to honor the cause of freedom.

"My mind and my knowledge of myself is formed by the victories that are the jewels in our African crown, the victories we earned from Isandhlwana to Khartoum, as Ethiopians and as the Ashanti of Ghana, as the Berbers of the desert.

"I am the grandchild who lays fresh flowers on the Boer graves at St Helena and the Bahamas, who sees in the mind's eye and suffers the suffering of a simple peasant folk, death, concentration camps, destroyed homesteads, a dream in ruins.

"I am the child of Nongqause. I am he who made it possible to trade in the world markets in diamonds, in gold, in the same food for which my stomach yearns.

"I come of those who were transported from India and China whose being resided in the fact, solely, that they were able to provide physical labour, who taught me that we could both be at home and be foreign, who taught me that human existence itself demanded that freedom was a necessary condition for that human existence.

"Being part of all these people, and in the knowledge that none dare contest that assertion, I shall claim – I am an African.

"I have seen our country torn asunder as these, all of whom are my people, engaged one another in a titanic battle, the one to redress a wrong that had been caused by one to another and the other, to defend the indefensible.

"I have seen what happens when one person has superiority of force over another, when the stronger appropriate to themselves the prerogative even to annul the injunction that God created all men and women in His image.

"I know what it signifies when race and color determine who is human and who is sub-human.

"I have seen the destruction of all sense of self-esteem, the consequent striving to be what one is not, simply to acquire some of the benefits, which those who had improved themselves as masters, had ensured that they enjoy.

"I have experience of the situation in which race and color enriches some and impoverishes the rest.

"I have seen concrete expression of the denial of the dignity of a human being emanating from the conscious, systemic and systematic oppressive and repressive activities of other human beings.

"There the victims parade with no mask to hide the brutish reality – the beggars, the prostitutes, the street children, those who seek solace in substance abuse, those who have to steal to assuage hunger, those who have to lose their sanity because to be sane is to invite pain.

"Perhaps the worst among these, who are my people, are those who have learnt to kill for a wage. To these the extent of death is directly proportional to their personal welfare.

"And so, like pawns in the service of demented souls, they kill in furtherance of the political violence in KwaZulu-Natal. They murder the innocent in the taxi wars. They kill slowly or quickly in order to make profits from the illegal trade in narcotics. They are available for hire when husband wants to murder wife and wife, husband.

"Among us prowl the products of our immoral and amoral past. Killers who have no sense of the worth of human life; rapists who have absolute disdain for the women of our country; animals who would seek to benefit from the vulnerability of the children; the disabled and the old; the rapacious who brook no obstacle in their quest for self-enrichment.

"All this I know and know to be true because I am an African! Because of that, I am also able to state the fundamental truth that I am born of a people who are heroes and heroines.

"I am born of a people who would not tolerate oppression. I am of a nation that would not allow fear of death, torture, imprisonment, exile or persecution in the perpetuation of injustice.

"The great masses who are our mothers and fathers will not permit that the behavior of the few results in the description of our country and peopleas barbaric.

"Patient because history is on their side, these masses do not despair because today the weather is bad, nor do they turn triumphalist when, tomorrow, the sun shines.

"Whatever the circumstances they have lived through and because of that experience, they are determined to define for themselves who they are and who they should be.

"We assemble here today to mark their victory in acquiring and exercising their right to formulate their own definition of what it means to be African.

"The constitution, whose adoption we celebrate, constitutes an unequivocal statement that we refuse to accept our Africanness as defined by race, color, gender or historical origins.

"It is a firm assertion made by us that South Africa belongs to all who live in it, black and white.

"It gives concrete expression to the sentiment we share as Africans, and will defend to the death, that the people shall govern.

"It recognizes the fact that the dignity of the individual is both an objective, which society must pursue, and a goal, which cannot be separate from the material well-being of that individual.

"It seeks to create the situation in which all our people shall be free from fear, including the fear of the oppression of one national group by another, the fear of the disempowerment of one social echelon by another, the fear of the use of state power to deny anybody their fundamental human rights and the fear of tyranny.

"It aims to open the doors so that those who were disadvantaged can assume their place in society as equals with their fellow human beings without regard to color, race, gender, age or geographic dispersal.

"It provides the opportunity to enable each and all to state their views, promote them, and strive for their implementation, in the process of governance without fear that a contrary view will meet with repression.

"It creates a law-governed society, which shall be inimical to arbitrary rule.

"It enables the resolution of conflicts by peaceful means rather than resorting to force. It rejoices in the diversity of our people and creates the space for all of us voluntarily to define ourselves as one people.

"As an African, I am proud, proud without reservation and proud without any feeling of conceit, of this achievement. Our sense of elevation at this moment also derives from the fact that this magnificent product is the unique creation of African hands and African minds.

"It also constitutes a tribute to our loss of vanity that we could, despite the temptation to treat ourselves as an exceptional fragment of humanity, draw on the accumulated experience and wisdom of all humankind to define for ourselves what we want to be.

"Together with the best in the world, we too are prone to pettiness, petulance, selfishness and shortsightedness. However, it seems to have happened that we looked at ourselves and said the time had come to make a super-human effort to be other than human, to respond to the call to create for ourselves a glorious future, to remind ourselves of the Latin saying: Gloria estconsequenda – Glory must be sought after!

"Today it feels good to be an African.

"It feels good to stand here as a South African, as a foot-soldier of a titanic African army, the African National Congress, to say to all the parties represented here, to the millions who made an input into the processes we are concluding, to our outstanding compatriots who have presided over the birth of our founding document, to the negotiators who pitted their wits one against the other, to the unseen stars who shone unseen as the management and administration of the Constitutional Assembly, the advisers, experts and publicists, to the mass communication media and to our friends across the globe – congratulations and well done!

"I am an African. I am born of the peoples of the continent of Africa.

"The pain of the violent conflict of the peoples of Liberia, Somalia, the Sudan, Burundi and Algeria is a pain I also bear.

"The dismal shame of poverty, suffering and human degradation of my continent is a blight that we share.

"The blight on our happiness that derives from this and from our drift to the periphery of the ordering of human affairs leaves us in a persistent shadow of despair. Nobody should be condemned to this savage road.

"This thing that we have done today, in this small corner of a great continent that has contributed so decisively to the evolution of humanity, says that Africa reaffirms that she is continuing her rise from the ashes. Whatever the setbacks of the moment, nothing can stop us now! Whatever the difficulties, Africa shall be at peace! However improbable it may sound to the skeptics, Africa will prosper!

"Whoever we may be, whatever our immediate interest, however much we carry baggage from our past, however much we have been caught by the fashion of cynicism and loss of faith in the capacity of the people, let us err today and say – nothing can stop us now!

"I am an African. Thank you"

THABO MBEKI
1996 Vice President, Republic of South Africa

Acknowledgements

Thank you to the following authors for providing further in sight pre- and post-Apartheid.

Adele Gould, the story of Nancy	www.adelgould.com
Ad and Wal	Peter Hain
Apartheid, the lighter side	Ben MacLennan
Day by Day Cartoons	Abe Berry, Star Newspaper, Johannesburg
Good Life, Good Death	Dr. Christiaan Barnard
Kaffir Boy	Mark Mathabane
Maids and Madams	Jacklyn Cock
Memorial Website for Helen Suzman	www.cortland.edu/cgis/ suzman

Miriam's Song	Miriam Mathabane and Mark Mathabane
Naught for Your Comfort	Trevor Huddleston
Playing the Enemy	John Carlin
Sugar Man – the life and death of Sixto Rodriguez	Stephen 'Sugar' Segerman
The Art of Coarse Rugby	Michael Green
You've Got To Be Carefully Taught	Richard Rodgers and Oscar Hammerstein II
	Copyright © 1949 by Richard Rodgers and Oscar Hammerstein II. Copyright Renewed. Williamson Music (ASCAP), an Imagem Company Owner of publication allied rights throughout the world. All Rights Reserved
The Disco Pants Blog	Susan Hayden, https://discopants